SHEBOYGAN COUNTY

"Partners in Progress" by Sylvia Bright Green

*Produced in cooperation with the Sheboygan
Area Chamber of Commerce*

*Windsor Publications, Inc.
Northridge, California*

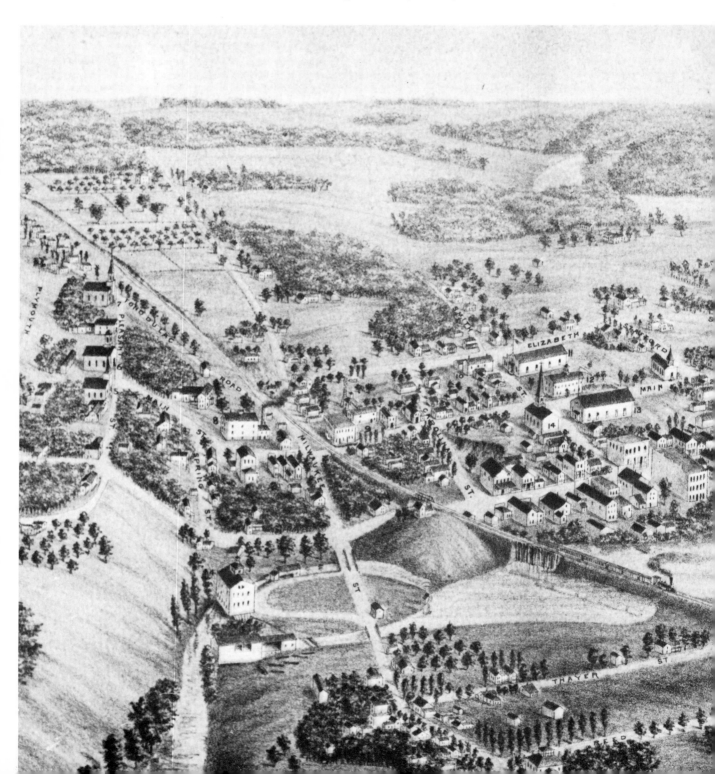

SHEBOYGAN COUNTY

150 Years of Progress

An Illustrated History by
Janice Hildebrand

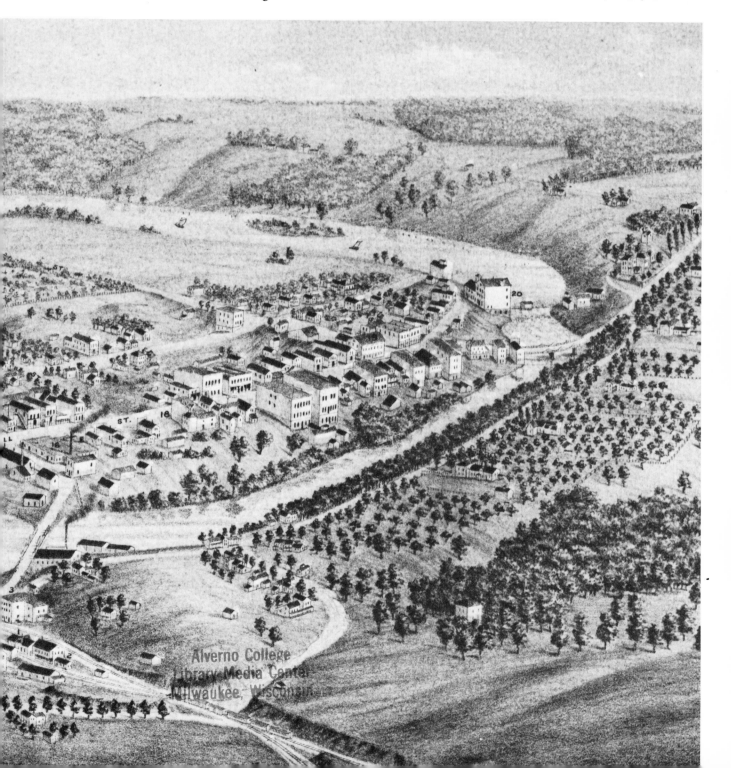

Windsor Publications, Inc.—History Books Division
Vice President of Publishing: Hal Silverman
Editorial Director: Teri Davis Greenberg
Design Director: Alex D'Anca
Corporate Biographies Director: Karen Story

Staff for *Sheboygan County*
Editor: Marilyn Horn
Photo Editor: Laura Cordova
Assistant Director, Corporate Biographies: Phyllis Gray
Editor, Corporate Biographies: Judith Hunter
Production Editor, Corporate Biographies: Una FitzSimons
Editorial Assistants: Didier Beauvoir, Brenda Berryhill, Michael Nugwynne, Kathy B.
  Peyser, Pat Pittman, Jeff Reeves, Theresa Solis
Proofreader: Susan J. Muhler
Layout Artist, Corporate Biographies: Mari Catherine Preimesberger
Sales Representative:r

Designer: Christina L. Rosepapa

Previous page: This rare 1855 photograph shows the Wade House in Greenbush, only six years after it was built. The Wade House was the most prominent stagecoach stop between Sheboygan and Fond du Lac. Today the refurbished building is preserved as a historic site by the state of Wisconsin. Courtesy, Old Wade House Collection

Facing page bottom: Sheboygan celebrated the nation's centennial in 1876 with street decorations and a May pole. This view of Eighth Street looking north from Pennsylvania Avenue includes the German Bank in the left hand corner building with George Groh's photographic studios and the Home Insurance Agency above it. Other businesses included are Nathan Cole Real Estate and the Wisconsin House. On the right corner is Feagan and Fairchild Grocery store. Courtesy, Sheboygan Press

CONTENTS

ACKNOWLEDGMENTS

The Sheboygan County Historical Research Center has been an invaluable resource in the writing of this book. I would like to thank its director Rose Rumpff for her support and encouragement, and Mary Meyer and Marilyn Payne for their help in finding, securing, and processing the photographs. Without their assistance this book would not have been possible.

A friendly Indian, Chief Solomon was a familiar sight to Sheboygan County residents. The Potawatomi lived near the Sheboygan Marsh, and Solomon regularly visited Plymouth, Sheboygan Falls, and Sheboygan, always receiving a generous handout from the residents. Courtesy, Sheboygan County Museum Collection

She-Boy-again!

Chapter I

THE BEGINNINGS OF A COUNTY

A fanciful tale often told to explain the derivation of the name "Sheboygan" concerns an Indian chief who had many sons but no daughters. When his wife presented him with another child she was supposed to have said, "She a boy again!" Courtesy, Sheboygan County Historical Research Center

Superbly situated on the western shore of Lake Michigan, Sheboygan County embraces approximately 521 square miles of gently rolling land. From the kettle moraine area in the western part of the county, known for its inland lakes, to the sand dunes and bluffs that border Lake Michigan, the countryside is a patchwork of rich Wisconsin farmland, small villages, scenic lakes, and streams. The land is well-watered by five different rivers—the Sheboygan, Pigeon, Mullett, Onion, and north branch of the Milwaukee.

Once the Indians—a mixture of Potawatomi, Chippewa, Ottawa, Winnebago, and Menominee—lived along the abundant rivers and lakes. The arrival of the fur trader, that swashbuckling, larger-than-life individual who opened the way for settlement of the West, marked the beginning of the end of the Indians' way of life.

Above: William Farnsworth, a Vermont native, settled in Wisconsin in 1818 when it was still a part of Michigan Territory. Considered the founder of Sheboygan County, he established a trading post along the Sheboygan River in 1820. A victim of the Lady Elgin *ship disaster in 1860, he was buried in Sheboygan's Wildwood Cemetery which is located on land he once owned.*

Right: The first home built in Sheboygan County was this log cabin erected by William Paine and Oliver Crocker in 1834. The two began a sawmill near William Farnsworth's Indian trading post on the Sheboygan River and lived near the site. They, however, failed to secure legal title to the land and lost it to Farnsworth in 1835. Courtesy, Sheboygan County Historical Research Center

Hunting for profit rather than need eventually led to the disappearance of the once-abundant game. Deprived of their chief source of livelihood, the Indians could only move northward as the pioneer settler followed the trader.

Jacques Vieau, father-in-law of Milwaukee settler Solomon Juneau, established a jack-knife trading post at "Shabouegan" in 1795. This post, mentioned in early writings concerning trade along the western shore of Lake Michigan, was one of a series of trading stops between Chicago and Mackinac that provided furs for the European trade. This setting proved to be an ideal outlet for the trapper's wares. The natural harbor where the Sheboygan River enters Lake Michigan is one of the finest along the lake. In addition, the river's headwaters form near Lake Winnebago, creating a natural trade route between Winnebago and Michigan. Indeed, one meaning for the Indian name "Sheboygan" is "waterway between the lakes."

SHEBOYGAN'S EARLY DEVELOPMENT

The first fur trader to establish a post and live in the area was William Farnsworth, regarded as the father of Sheboygan County. Born in Vermont on September 26, 1796, Farnsworth moved to Canada and then to Wisconsin, settling in the Green Bay district about 1818 and began working for the American Fur Company. His marriage to Queen Marinette (Marie Antoinette Chevailer) of the Menominee Indians resulted in a prosperous trade. He established his trading post at Sheboygan in 1820. In 1833, when the Indians of Wisconsin were forced to vacate their lands to the federal government, Queen Marinette divorced him in order to protect her lands and her people.

Two of their three children, George and Joe, remained with their father and figured prominently in the settlement of the county. Farnsworth was to marry twice more, losing both wives and a daughter to death. Queen Marinette died in Green Bay in 1865.

In the summer of 1834 Oliver Crocker, a New Yorker, and William Paine, an Englishman, built a sawmill and log cabin near Farnsworth's trading post at the first rapids of the Sheboygan River. However, the two men had failed to secure legal title to the land, and in 1835 Farnsworth purchased the property and closed his trading post.

He engaged Jonathan Follett and his wife Eliza to take charge of the mill. Mrs. Follett, the first white woman to reside in the county, ran a boardinghouse and hostelry for the mill hands and the occasional passing traveler. Farnsworth owned the mill for 10 years, then sold it to Samuel Ormsbee in 1845.

Farnsworth was an active participant in the early development of Sheboygan. A land speculator, town promoter, and businessman, he was a candidate for village president and for first mayor in 1853, both times losing to Henry Conklin, early merchant of Sheboygan. Farnsworth also served as a commissioner of the Sheboygan and Fond du Lac Railway in 1847 and of the reincorporated Sheboygan and Mississippi Railroad in 1852. He was a member of the board when the village was incorporated in 1846, and he served as a fire warden in 1855.

Although he maintained his home in Sheboygan, Farnsworth's interests were not restricted to this county. He was either a partner in or owned two sailing ships, the *Jefferson* and the *Traveler*, as well as a store in Green Bay.

Active and powerful, Farnsworth was not the kind of man to die in bed. His death was in keeping with his adventurous life. On September 8, 1860, he was aboard the ill-fated steamer, the *Lady Elgin*, when the ship was rammed by the schooner *Augusta* during a storm on Lake Michigan. His body washed ashore near Evanston, Illinois, and was sent to Sheboygan for interment on September 12. According to the local newspaper, the *Evergreen City Times*, his remains were followed to the grave by the largest procession seen in the city. Obsequies were conducted by the Freemasons of Sheboygan and Sheboygan Falls, and the procession of carriages was led by the uniformed German Rifle Company and Protection Fire Company No. 1.

One of the many men that Farnsworth induced to settle in Sheboygan was Charles D. Cole. Born in Schenectady, New York, in 1806, Cole was an enterprising and ambitious man. By the time he was 16 years old, he was captain of a canal boat on the Erie Canal.

Charles D. Cole, a distinguished citizen of Sheboygan County, was instrumental in convincing many New Yorkers to immigrate to the county, including his mother, sisters, brothers, and his wife's family. He was an early postmaster at Sheboygan and Sheboygan Falls, an Indian trader and store owner, farmer, financier, government land agent, registrar of deeds, and the founder of the first Temperance Society in Wisconsin. From the Illustrated Historical Atlas of Sheboygan County, Wisconsin, *1902*

Sarah Trowbridge Cole, wife of Charles Trowbridge, was a true pioneer woman. She moved to Sheboygan in 1836 with two young children, and was forced to camp out along the banks of the Sheboygan River while the Sheboygan House, the settlement's first hotel, was being constructed. She then moved to Sheboygan Falls in 1839 and taught the first local school in her home. From the Illustrated Historical Atlas of Sheboygan County, Wisconsin, 1902

He later moved to Cleveland, Ohio, where he became the owner of several boats on the Ohio Canal and where in 1831 he married Sarah Trowbridge, a daughter of Deacon William and Dorothy Chapin Trowbridge.

The mid-1830s were a time of wild speculation and westward expansion in the United States. Eastern businessmen were pouring money into unseen parcels of land in the territories hoping to make their fortunes. Cole was one of the many entrepreneurs who traveled west seeking greater opportunities. En route to Chicago in 1836, after disposing of his boats, he met Farnsworth, who encouraged him to set up a store and forwarding business in Sheboygan. Cole and Farnsworth traveled to Chicago together to purchase land at the mouth of the Sheboygan River. The following remarks were made by Cole regarding the scene in Chicago:

Unbounded excitement about real estate. Everybody crazy. An old gentleman of African persuasion used to ride a horse through the tourists ringing a bell and crying now's your time to make your fortune. Everybody stayed at the Tremont, a frame building kept as a hotel for tourists. At meal time the rush was unparalleled, it exceeded the rush for the auctioneer stand.

After purchasing land Cole and Farnsworth hired Asahel G. Dye to construct a dock and warehouse, the first commercial establishments located on the present site of the city of Sheboygan. Dye and the Morris Farmin family became the first residents of Sheboygan. Before the 160-foot dock and the 40- by-60-foot warehouse were completed, Cole returned to Cleveland to bring his wife and sons, George and William, to their new home.

William Ashby, another '36er, was hired by Farnsworth to work at the mill. A native of New York, Ashby remained in the county for the rest of his life. Farnsworth also hired Levi Conroe, a mechanic, Elihu Thorp, and several other workmen to erect the Sheboygan House, which became the temporary home for every arrival in the new settlement. The Sheboygan House, the warehouse, and Dye's house were the only buildings in Sheboygan in 1836. The hotel was destroyed by fire in 1850.

In September 1836 Cole opened his stock of goods in the Sheboygan House under the name of C.D. Cole & Co. The following May 25, 1837, his son James Riley was born, the first white child born in the county.

Benjamin Gibbs, a tailor, came in the fall of 1836 to settle in the county, and was soon joined by his two brothers, John and James. The three men purchased land and began farms in the town of Lima. Their settlement became known as Gibbsville.

Wisconsin became a territory in 1836. Henry Dodge was appointed governor and on November 25 Charles Cole was named postmaster at Sheboygan. Sheboygan County was established on December 7, 1836, by an act of the territorial legislature, which detached it from Brown County except for judicial purposes. Levi Conroe was appointed justice of the peace by Governor Dodge.

Farnsworth, in partnership with several others, platted the village of Sheboygan in 1836 and proceeded to sell lots. About 200 lots had been sold and an estimated 17 buildings erected by 1838. Prices of these lots ranged from several hundred to several thousand dollars.

The *Green Bay Intelligencer*, Wisconsin's first newspaper, reported on March 2, 1836:

Sac Creek, Sheboygan, Sleeping River and Manitowoc are at this moment the rage. At the Sheboygan, the most beautiful, and we doubt not the most important town on the Lake the property has risen to an enormous height. A company of purchasers are laying out a thousand or more town lots, and will have them offered for sale in a short time.

Near Farnsworth's mill, Follett laid out 33 acres for building purposes. Hopes were high that Sheboygan would soon outgrow Milwaukee and become the metropolis of Wisconsin. Its location, halfway between Green Bay and the southern boundary of the territory, seemed most advantageous. What the people neglected to realize was that the country surrounding Sheboygan was a vast unbroken forest. After building their homes and businesses, there was nothing they could do but await the expected arrival of more settlers.

General prosperity prevailed throughout the United States during the mid-1830s. This was the era of internal improvements; of building canals, railroads, and roads involving excessive extension of credit by banks and large-scale borrowing by state governments. It also led to the establishment of numerous lesser institutions for banking purposes. These "banks," by issuing a redundancy of paper money, served not only to enhance prices but also to stimulate speculation. Much of this circulating money issued proved to be entirely worthless. Yet confidence prevailed, encouraging an unparalleled speculation in Western lands.

THE PANIC OF 1837

The bubble was to burst shortly. In 1837 Congress refused to renew the charter of the Bank of the United States. This caused an outburst

In August 1893 Alexis Clermont donned the same buckskin suit he had worn some 60 years earlier as a mail carrier between Chicago and Green Bay. The World's Fair was opening at Chicago in September and Clermont wished to repeat his mail route of 1825-1830, in the same manner as he had done before, on foot. As a young man accompanied by an Oneida Indian and following an obscure trail through the wilderness of Wisconsin, the 500-mile round trip took him a month to complete. At the age of 85, he walked ten miles each day, attracting attention wherever he traveled. Brass bands gave him a welcome as he passed through each town. He sold this photograph as he tramped along. Courtesy, Ray Van Handel, Jr.

Silas Stedman was 51 years old when he founded the city of Sheboygan Falls in 1835. Having served in the militia in his native Massachusetts, he retained a military bearing and was an excellent horseman. His fellow citizens knew him as a kindly, courteous gentleman who was fair in all his dealings. From the Illustrated Historical Atlas of Sheboygan County, Wisconsin, *1902*

of fear—many banks closed, businesses failed, and industry was paralyzed. Some states repudiated bonds issued for the payment of improvements. The resulting depression lasted eight years.

The winter of 1836-1837 proved disastrous for the Wisconsin territory, particularly for the new settlement at Sheboygan. Provisions became scarce in the fall. The ship sent by Farnsworth to supply the village was unable to land because of a storm. By December the stores of food at Sheboygan, Farnsworth's mill, and at Rochester (Sheboygan Falls) were almost depleted.

Cole borrowed a yoke of oxen from Farnsworth's mill and started to Milwaukee for provisions. Ashby and several men from the mill accompanied him on the trip, which took seven days through the unbroken forests. Cole described the return:

Our purchases consisted of corn, oats, flour, some groceries . . . We encamped one night at or near the present village of Sackville. We had arranged for spending the night as comfortable as possible. We had not slept long before we were aroused by our oxen. They had broken into our provisions and had filled themselves so full of corn that we were greatly alarmed for their safety. We at once yoked them up, attached them to the sled and started, hoping to save their lives by exercising them pretty briskly, but they had overgorged and one of them paid the penalty of his indiscretion with his life.

The small stock of provisions did not last long, and Cole was only home a few days before he started for Green Bay on horseback to secure more food. He was to spend most of the winter traveling between Sheboygan and Green Bay for supplies.

Summer brought little relief to the settlements in the county. Cole again supplied them by going to Milwaukee in a birch bark canoe. His trips became so numerous that Milwaukee settlers dubbed his transportation company the "Sheboygan Express." In reminiscing about these events, Cole wrote:

We were often pinched for food, and at one time we dug up and ate the potatoes we had put in the ground for an increase, and at another, we cut the hoops and staves off a barrel of condemned flour that had mildewed and become hard, and was rolled under the warehouse to be out of the way; this flour we pounded up with a hatchet, and made it into bread or something we called such.

The dreams of new homes in the wilderness were becoming nightmares. Settlers abandoned Sheboygan. Those who still had a little money mounted their homes on rafts and had them towed to

Milwaukee. Others quietly disappeared, but most of the residents moved to the interior of the county, settling in or near Sheboygan Falls. By the end of 1839 Sheboygan was deserted except for the James Farnsworth family.

RECOVERY AND REBIRTH

In October 1835 a courtly gentleman from Springfield, Massachusetts, Silas Stedman, arrived at Farnsworth's mill in search of land to purchase and develop. Following the river westward from the mill, he camped overnight some five miles away. In the morning he became aware of the sound of falling water and, following the sound, came upon the falls of the Sheboygan River. The river was, at that time, wide and swiftly moving, cascading over rapids and rock ledges. Stedman immediately realized the potential of the waterpower and determined to buy the site.

Traveling to Green Bay to purchase the property at the government land sale in November 1835, he formed a partnership with several other men who wished to buy the same land. With the land secured, Stedman contracted to have a sawmill built and returned to Massachusetts to bring his wife to the site.

Stedman was not the usual pioneer settler. He was born in Chicopee, Massachusetts, in 1785, the son of Phineas Stedman, a Revolutionary War soldier, and Sarah Howard. Early in life he developed a taste for the military and gained the rank of colonel in the militia. He served one term in the Massachusetts legislature. In 1825 he married Elizabeth Bolles, a daughter of Deacon Nathan and Elizabeth Howard Bolles. The two had no children, and perhaps this is what prompted Stedman at the age of 51, when most men were content to stay at home, to seek new opportunities in the West.

Upon his return to the falls, Stedman, finding that the mill had

Above: Elizabeth Bolles Stedman, wife of Silas Stedman, was a quiet, unassuming woman who followed her husband into the wilderness of Wisconsin in 1836. Contemporaries remember her as being well-groomed and never without a dainty lace cap tied around her head. From the Illustrated Historical Atlas of Sheboygan County, Wisconsin, *1902*

Below: The ramshackle appearance of Stedman's sawmill belies the fact that it once was the center of industry in Sheboygan Falls. Swept away in the flood of 1883, the building housed the beginnings of many industries in the city. Courtesy, Sheboygan County Historical Research Center

not been built, contacted Levi Conroe to build it as quickly as possible. Lumber was selling at a high price and it was to his advantage to begin manufacturing without delay. However, the mill was not finished until December, and navigation had closed so no lumber could be sold that year.

Stedman's mill was a two-story frame building mounted upon log supports that rested on the bedrock of the river. In one corner of the sawmill, Stedman installed a set of stones for grinding flour and grist. For the next several years there was not enough grain raised in the county to keep it running, although the set of stones supplied flour for the people in what is now Fond du Lac, Manitowoc, Calumet, Ozaukee, Washington, and Kewaunee counties. The mill was swept away in the flood of 1883, but during its lifetime housed many diverse industries of Sheboygan Falls such as the Quinlan Rake, the Mattoon Chair Spindle, the Taylor Brothers Sash, Door and Blind factories, and the Prentice Woolen Mills.

The exodus from Sheboygan benefited Sheboygan Falls most directly by bringing the Cole family to the village. On April 8, 1839, Cole resigned his position as postmaster and moved to Sheboygan Falls, which at that time was called Rochester. When the territorial legislature authorized the first election of county officials in December 1838, Cole was elected register of deeds. On January 11, 1840, he was appointed postmaster of the village, effectively making Sheboygan Falls the county seat.

Cole was also appointed receiver of the U.S. Land Office at Green Bay, his district covering half the territory of Wisconsin. In a private capacity he was also a land agent, Indian trader, farmer, sawmill operator, lumberyard owner, founder of the first Temperance Society in the state, and an organizer of the Sheboygan and Fond du Lac Plank Road and the Sheboygan and Mississippi Railroad.

Charles Cole, a full-time Sheboygan County booster, was probably responsible for bringing more settlers to the county than anyone else excepting Farnsworth. The first of these were his in-laws, the Trowbridges, and five of their eight children. They followed Cole to Sheboygan in 1837. Deacon Trowbridge, a whitesmith and manufacturer of edged tools, conducted a blacksmith shop in Sheboygan that year. They, too, moved to Sheboygan Falls, settling on a farm west of the village.

Shortly thereafter they were joined by their son Benjamin and his wife, Charity Rounseville. In 1840 their daughter Lucy and her husband, Albert Rounseville, followed. Within a few more years they were joined by Deacon Trowbridge's brother Elijah, his wife, Eliza Ann Cutting, their eight children, and the sons of another brother,

Dr. James Trowbridge.

In addition to the Trowbridges, Cole brought his mother, his brother George, and sisters Mary, Sarah, and Clara to the Falls after the death of his father in 1842. During the next three years his brothers, Amos, William, and John Beekman, followed.

While Sheboygan Falls slowly grew and prospered, Sheboygan was dormant. Few settlers arrived at the port. In 1840 Alva Rublee arrived with his family to co-manage Farnsworth's mill along with Adonikim Farrow. Rublee's son Horace remembered his first morning in Sheboygan:

The morning showed a strange spectacle. Scattered about through the pleasant groves of second-growth pine and oak, which covered the plat, were well-built houses neatly painted and new; and along several streets were a number of buildings, designed for stores, all abandoned.

In 1842 George C. Cole listed every resident in the county:

At Sheboygan and along the lake: Captain N.W. Brooks, wife and girl; Stephen Wolverton, wife, son, and daughter; Joshua Brown and wife; John Glass and wife; Don Fairchild; David Wilson and family; Alvah Rublee and family; David Evans and wife; Hiram G.D. Squires; William Ashby and wife; Aaron Ritter and family; A. Farrow and Wentworth Barber.

The Dye settlement: Asahel G. Dye and family; the widow Farmin and son Benjamin; Newell Upham and wife; Chauncey Hall and family; Wendell Hoffman and wife; Elizabeth Cady and brother Edward.

Gibbsville: John D. Gibbs and wife; Benjamin L. Gibbs and wife; John Johnson, wife, sons George, Michael, Robert, John, and William, and daughters Ann and Maria; Peter Palmer and wife; William Palmer; Leroy Palmer; Allen W. Knight and wife.

Sheboygan Falls: Albert Rounseville, wife, and two children; Benjamin C. Trowbridge, wife, and family, including Alvira O'Cain and Maria Dieckmann; Seth Morse; Samuel Rounseville; Harmon Pierce; Nelson Bradford; George O. Trowbridge; Silas Stedman and wife; David Giddings and wife; Charles D. Cole, wife, and family; Chloe Cole and family; William Trowbridge, wife, and sons William S., James T., Thaddeus, and John.

The early settlers formed the nucleus of the county. They remained to log the forests, clear and farm the land, build homes, schools, and churches, and establish the industries that provided employment for the rush of newcomers that would begin to arrive in 1845.

Chapter II

YANKEES, IMMIGRANTS, AND THE CIVIL WAR

Singing has always played an important part in German life. On February 9, 1860, these men founded the Concordia to promote German singing and German social life. Courtesy, Concordia Singing Society

The decade from 1845 to 1855 witnessed a second wave of settlement in Sheboygan County. Land-hungry New Englanders, anxious to shake off the shackles of their older cities and taste the excitement of the West, comprised the bulk of settlers, as they had in 1836. In addition, hundreds and then thousands of foreign immigrants touched Sheboygan's shore, making it a stepping-off spot for settlement of the county, Wisconsin, and states farther west.

Although only 227 people populated the county in 1842, by 1846 the population numbered 4,637, and by 1850, 8,836. The Wisconsin *Gazetteer*, published in 1853, stated that there were 1,790 dwellings, 581 farms, and 30 manufactures in the county.

Why did these young families leave their settled homes in the

East? Daniel Hyatt of Plymouth explained it this way in a letter to his parents in Stanfordville, New York, in January 1850:

I do not know of anything that would induce me to come back . . . aside from the association of family ties . . . Your rules of society with its codfish aristocracy is enough to disgust the independence of a Western man to say nothing of stuck up noses of the folks that ape riches with silk and broadcloth . . .

There is more independence in setting down in your own house eating bread raised on one's own farm than this transient trapping around the world and I venture to predict you would enjoy life better in Wisconsin than you ever have in that place with all its codfish aristocracy high life associations. There is more sympathy in a community where there is no rivalry, where all are on an equality except as regards morals.

Now what is this cry about leaving a good country and coming to a new one? What are all those hardships so much talked about? They amount to a few kinds of fruit, oysters and such dainties that a Badger's stomach do not need nor appetite require.

BY LAND AND BY WATER: IMMIGRANTS COME TO SHEBOYGAN

Immigrants came to Sheboygan County by two different routes: via the Great Lakes, the preferred method, and overland south of the Great Lakes. Buffalo, New York, situated on the western terminal of the Erie Canal and the New York and Erie Railway, was the great starting place for the majority of Wisconsin-bound settlers. There, ships took on their passengers to make the three-week trip to Wisconsin. In a letter written on April 30, 1878, Lucy Trowbridge Rounseville described her trip to Sheboygan Falls in 1840:

In the spring of 1840 my husband, Albert Rounseville closed up his business in Caroline, New York preparatory to emigrating to Wisconsin. Mr. Charles D. Cole, my brother-in-law, in 1836, and my father Deacon William Trowbridge in 1837, having led the way to this "Eldorado of the West." Benjamin Trowbridge, my eldest brother, who came in the spring of 1837 . . . returned on business and to escort us on our way.

On the 16th of May, we left our old home and at night had engaged passage and removed our effects on a canal boat bound for Buffalo

. . . Arrived at Buffalo, we again took passage on the brig Erie, *as no steamers at that time would land passengers at Sheboygan. It was our misfortune to have for our captain a raw material, making his first trip in that capacity, and totally unacquainted with the channels; and although having competent officers, he was too conceited to heed their advice, and consequently we ran aground in Saginaw Bay and had to be lighted off by a schooner. Head winds, severe storms and mismanagement detained us and we were obliged to put up at Big Beaver Island and await more prosperous gales. While at this island, our provisions, which were nearly exhausted, were doled out to each of the crew and passengers in shares, subject to each individual's judgment.*

On the morning of the 18th of June, as luck would have it, we landed at the mouth of the long-looked-for Sheboygan River.

The alternative route—overland south of the Great Lakes —allowed families to take along more of their possessions but was even slower than traveling by water. Roads were bad or nonexistent. The animals had to be rested frequently and could only cover 15 to 25 miles per day.

There were no roads in Sheboygan County until the military road connecting Green Bay and Chicago was completed by the government in 1839. Little work was done on this road except to cut the brush and trees along the right-of-way. It was used mainly in winter, as Lake Michigan's water route was safer, quicker, and easier during the other months. Through the efforts of David Giddings, who surveyed the route from Manitowoc Rapids to Port Washington without compensation, the road was routed through Sheboygan Falls, where the government also built the first bridge over the river.

Although built for military purposes, the Green Bay road was important to the development of the county, it being the only route to the northern part of the county. This was the road traveled by the "Lippers," who settled in the town of Herman in 1847. Their trip was a long and arduous one. A group of single men and men with families from the Lippe-Detmold area of Germany left Bremen for the United States on May 4, 1847, under the leadership of Friedrich Reineking. The eight-week passage was one of misery and hardship. Their sailing vessel, the *Agnes*, was crowded and overloaded, resulting in three deaths.

Scheduled to land at New York, the ship landed at Quebec instead. The Lippers, as they came to be known, traveled by ship, canal boat, and train to Buffalo, then boarded a steamer for Milwaukee en route to their destination of Iowa. Land agents in Milwaukee

This log homestead was built by Frederick Horneck and his son Philip in 1850 when they settled in the town of Rhine. Descendants of the family were still living here in 1898 when this photograph was taken. A porch has been added to the front of the log cabin since then, and a productive vegetable garden is visible in the front of the house. Courtesy, Janice Strange Bub

painted a bleak picture of the prairies of Iowa and encouraged them to stay in Wisconsin. Unable to agree, the group divided, with some going to Iowa and the majority going on to Sheboygan County. Traveling the government road to the northern part of the county, they ended their journey on July 25, 1847, settling in the town of Herman.

The Lippers were not the first Germans to settle in the county, however. In the spring of 1845 four young men started farms in the town of Sheboygan Falls: George Thiermann, Diedrich Barthels, N. Heide, and Diedrich Longeman.

These families from Germany proved to be the advance wave of immigrants. After the political trials of 1848, Germans fled their country by the thousands, and by 1860 there were 10,284 German-born residents in the county.

Residents from the Netherlands also began arriving in the county in 1845. The first to arrive were Jan Zeeveld and Leunis De-Vos, who settled in the town of Holland. In the summer of 1847 a group under the leadership of the Reverend Peter Zonne also homesteaded in Holland.

THE VOYAGE OF THE *PHOENIX*

Zonne's group was a forerunner of another group to arrive in the fall. These immigrants from the Dutch provinces of Gelderland and

Overijssel left Rotterdam at the end of September. They reached New York a month later and traveled to Buffalo, where they boarded the *Phoenix,* a two-year-old, 302-ton wooden ship powered by a steam-driven propeller. She also carried a mast so that sails could be rigged if the propeller failed. This, the last scheduled voyage of the winter for the *Phoenix,* proved to be her last.

Accounts of the disaster that befell the ship differ. The known facts are that Captain B.G. Sweet fell and broke his leg when the ship was near Cleveland, Ohio, on November 13. Confined to his stateroom for the rest of the voyage, he could not directly oversee his crew.

The ship arrived at Manitowoc on November 20 to unload freight and take on wood for the boiler. Survivors of the *Phoenix* would later report that the crew had gotten drunk at their brief stop and let the boiler run dry.

For whatever reason, fire broke out in the boiler room about 4 P.M. Efforts to contain the blaze were futile and the ship was quickly engulfed in flames. The *Phoenix* was within five miles of Sheboygan and all thought turned to the ship's three small lifeboats, scarcely adequate to carry the 300-odd passengers. The lifeboats were launched with the idea of quickly rowing to shore and returning for the others. Captain Sweet was put into one boat and a crew member in each of the others. One boat capsized almost immediately. In the resulting confusion and panic, one of the oars of another boat was lost and the boat had to be sculled ashore. The two surviving lifeboats carried 43 people, who bailed water with their wooden shoes. When the nearly frozen survivors finally reached

This group of Holland pioneers gathered to have their picture taken in July 1897 to celebrate the 50th anniversary of the Holland settlement in Sheboygan County. Typical Dutch names of the group included Obrink, Bruggink, Heslink, Mentink, Roerdink, Wilterdink, and Vrugink. Photo by William Bub

shore, Captain Sweet ordered a fire to be built.

Back aboard the *Phoenix*, people tried to evade the flames by climbing the rigging and the mast. Others tried to build rafts, hoping to cling to them until the lifeboats returned. But the fire continued to rage and one by one the victims were consumed by fire or jumped into the icy lake.

On shore, Judge Morris arose early that Sunday morning. From his home overlooking Sheboygan's North Point, he saw the burning ship. Racing to the harbor, he awoke the crews of two ships, the *Delaware* and the *Liberty*. The *Delaware* had a steam-powered propellor and it took some time to fire up her boilers. The *Liberty* was a schooner and there was no wind for her sails.

The news of the tragedy spread quickly, and residents lined the shore to watch the drama unfold. They could see the people leaping into the water from the ship. They also saw the bonfire north of the village that Captain Sweet had ordered to be built. Wagons were immediately sent to aid the survivors.

By the time the *Delaware* arrived on the scene, the *Phoenix* had burned to the waterline. Only three of the crew members—two clinging to the anchor chains and one floating with a piece of debris —could be found. The *Delaware* towed the ship to Sheboygan and tied her to the north pier. Within days residents of Milwaukee and neighboring communities were taking up collections in churches or attending a meeting to consider ways to aid the 46 survivors, 25 of whom were from Holland.

Historians agree that the disaster was a strong deterrent to further Dutch immigration to Wisconsin. The victims, mostly prominent men and women in the Netherlands, had come with money to purchase land and to buy stock and provisions. After the catastrophe rumors spread that $500,000 of the settlers' gold lay buried at the bottom of the lake. In 1894 a group of investors from Detroit, Michigan, organized an expedition to salvage the gold. Nothing ever came of the scheme and the final resting place of the gold remains a mystery today.

One story was circulated about Jimmy Berry, an enterprising young man who searched the still-smoldering remains of the *Phoenix* and dug out some melted gold and jewels. Supposedly he used it to purchase two milk cows from a farmer in Ohio.

A contemporary of the time, Laura Chase Smith, in an 1847 letter to her grandfather, Bishop Philander Chase, gave her version of the tragedy:

You have probably heard the particulars of the dreadful calamity of the burning of the Phoenix. *It is said to be the result of the grossest carelessness on the part of the engineers and firemen. I think there were only 47 saved out of nearly 300. I saw the yet burning wreck as it was towed in shore by the* Delaware. *Nothing can be more aggravating than all the circumstances. They could have been saved had there been steam to carry them in shore only 5 miles distant. The* Delaware *lay anchored near this place, and hastened to their relief on the first bursting out of the flames, and came ever so near that the shrieks of the sufferers were heard but on arrival at the scene of the fire only three were picked up alive, two hanging to the cable chains and one upon some fragments. Five dead bodies were picked up and 47 steerage passengers went ashore in the small boats. 250 human beings had perished in one short hour either by fire or flood and no bodies have as yet been recovered except the five on the morning of the disaster.*

Efforts to erect a memorial to commemorate one of the worst shipping disasters in the history of the Great Lakes have been ongoing since the tragedy, but as of 1988 they remained unfulfilled.

IRISH SETTLERS ARRIVE

The first Irish family arrived in the county in May 1846. John O'Reilly, with his four sons from County Mearth, was followed by the Fritz brothers, the Humphreys, and the Seekins, and settled in the town of Mitchell. By 1848 a wave of Irish immigrants crossed the Atlantic to America because of the potato crop failure and the resulting famine. Some of these families settled in the Mitchell area.

Mitchell and Lyndon were one large township until 1850, when they were separated. Mitchell was at first called Olio (which means a wide-mouthed earthen pot) because a large part of the land lies in the kettle moraine area with its peculiar bowl-like valleys. In 1851 the name was changed to Mitchell to honor the Irish patriot John Mitchell for his efforts to relieve the sufferings of his countrymen. By 1860, 100 of the 175 families living in Mitchell were Irish.

THE FOURIER SETTLEMENTS

Preceding the Irish were Yankee settlers intrigued with the idea of Fourierism. A French clerk, Francois Marie Charles Fourier, wrote a book entitled *The Social Destiny of Man: Or Theory of the Four Movements* in 1808. Briefly, Fourier's social theory stated that a natural social order exists corresponding to Newton's ordering of the universe and that both evolved in eight ascending periods. In the highest stage, created by dividing society into phalanges, man's emotions would be freely expressed.

The phalange was to be a cooperative agricultural community

bearing responsibility for the social welfare of the individual and characterized by continual shifting of roles among its members. Phalanges, which could be introduced into any political system, supposedly would distribute wealth more equitably than under capitalism.

Cooperatives based on Fourier's ideas were started in France and quickly spread to the United States. One of Fourierism's chief advocates in this country was Horace Greeley, who popularized the concept in his newspaper. The best-known of the American cooperatives were Brook Farm in Massachusetts and the North American Phalanx at Red Bank, New Jersey.

A large number of New Englanders settling in Wisconsin brought these ideas with them. A Wisconsin phalanx was formed in Southport (Kenosha) during the winter of 1843-1844 and moved to Ceresco, now a part of Ripon, in May 1844. Two less-famous phalanxes were formed in Sheboygan County, the first of which was the Spring Farm Settlement in Mitchell Township.

One of the early disciples of Fourierism was Charles Cole. In a letter to John Beekman on February 16, 1845, he asked his brother if he was favorable to the cause, hinting at a project that would "fill you with ecstacy." On April 13 he elaborated on his plan:

The facts of the case is this—there is several of the first men in this place—amongst which is Col Stedman, Father Trowbridge and the rest are as good men who are favorable to the Theory. And they with myself have concluded that if all things proves favorable and our means are sufficient and the right kind of persons can be associated with us, that we will, at some future time, go into association for farming and other purposes.

But apparently John Beekman was not in favor of the Fourierites.

In the same letter, Mary Cole, their sister, wrote that their mother

thinks she has grown better since she found out you were no Fourierite. She had been going down hill—worse than ever since Charles joined them . . . She began to think they were all foresaking her.

Ten families (without the Coles) met to form a Fourierite community, but they could not agree on a location. The resulting split caused two communities to be formed: the Spring Farm Settlement and the Pigeon River Colony.

The latter colony, founded in 1847, was situated upon the bluffs of the Pigeon River north of Sheboygan. Among the families who settled at Pigeon River were Newton Goodell's and William Seaman's. The families lived in separate log shanties which were built five feet apart with all property commonly owned. They planted crops for two seasons, but in both years the crops failed. Hunger, perhaps more than anything, caused the demise of the experiment in 1849.

Under the leadership of Benjamin Trowbridge, the remaining families established the Spring Farm Settlement in Mitchell in the spring of 1846. They included Albert Rounseville, James Trowbridge, John Sanborn, Daniel Sanborn, and James O'Cain. In September they were joined by James Angus, John Hurn, John Smith, E.L. Adams, and Alfred Launsdale. Horace Greeley visited the phalanx in July 1847 and found that a community house had been started and 30 acres of land were under cultivation.

The group petitioned the territorial legislature to grant them a charter under the name "Spring Farm Phalanx." Harrison Hobart was charged with obtaining the necessary papers, but under the leadership of Marshall Strong of Racine, who was opposed to all reform groups, the legislature denied the request.

The Spring Farm experiment lasted three years, but was doomed to failure without the charter from the legislature. The group dissolved with most of the families leaving the area.

TOLL ROADS OPEN WESTERN SETTLEMENT

The years between 1848 and 1855 were the era of the plank (or toll) roads. Many different roads were proposed but only two were actually built. The most important of these was the Fond du Lac road, which opened the settlement of the western part of the country and provided the village of Fond du Lac with an outlet to Lake Michigan. The other plank road was the Calumet, which ran in a northwesterly direction through Calumet County.

With the advent of the plank roads, stagecoach lines were established, and, at the height of their popularity, Sheboygan was the center of four stage routes: north to Manitowoc, west to Fond du Lac, southwest to Cascade, and south to Milwaukee. With the establishment of stagecoach routes, the need arose for lodging, food, and way stations. One of the most prominent of these taverns, which were found every four or five miles on the toll roads, was the Wade House at Greenbush.

Sylvanus Wade migrated north from Joliet, Illinois, in the spring of 1844 with his family, becoming the first settlers of Greenbush. Their first home, a log cabin where food and sleeping accommodations were provided to travelers, was known as the Half Way House

Massachusetts-born Sylvanus Wade traveled by wagon to Joliet, Illinois, in 1836 with his wife Betsy and their nine children. In 1844 the family settled in the town of Greenbush in Sheboygan County, and established the Wade House, a famous tavern on the Sheboygan-Fond du Lac Plank Road. Courtesy, Old Wade House Collection

Above: This wood-burning locomotive used to make regular runs on the Sheboygan to Fond du Lac railroad. Courtesy, Sheboygan Press

Right: This rare 1855 photograph shows the Wade House in Greenbush, only six years after it was built. The Wade House was the most prominent stagecoach stop between Sheboygan and Fond du Lac. Today the refurbished building is preserved as a historic site by the state of Wisconsin. Courtesy, Old Wade House Collection

because of its location halfway between Sheboygan and Fond du Lac. In 1849 the present Wade House, now preserved as a historic site by the State of Wisconsin, was opened. A large and pretentious inn for its era, the Wade House is a famous landmark of the county.

Another famous inn was the Farmers' Inn, run by Jane Johnson of Gibbsville. Begun shortly after Mrs. Johnson settled there with her husband John in 1837, the tavern became a favorite stopping place for travelers on the government road between Chicago and Green Bay. A native of Yorkshire, England, Jane was said to have superior qualities for a landlady. The Farmers' Inn gained the reputation of being the most comfortable and homelike stopping place on the government road. It was said that no wayfarer was ever refused a good meal or a night's lodging for lack of money.

The end of the plank roads era came with the building of the railroads. In 1863 the state legislature passed a law stating that when any part of a plank road was abandoned by failure to make repairs or collect tolls for a period of 60 days, it would be deemed a public highway. The last toll road in the county was abandoned in 1902.

SHEBOYGAN IN THE 1850s

By 1850 Sheboygan was growing into a thriving commercial center. Pennsylvania Avenue, the main street, was lined with business buildings from the pier on Lake Michigan west to Ninth Street. The Gibbs Hotel, operated by the Gibbs brothers, was the social center for men and women from the Eastern states (called "Yankees" to distinguish them from the foreign-born). It was also the starting point for stagecoaches until the railroad was completed to Fond du Lac in 1869. The first saleable products of the county, after the logging industry, were whitefish and shingles. Shingles were bundled and tied for shipping; whitefish had to be barreled and cooperages were begun. Potash soon became an export as farmers burned the brush and trees from the virgin land and hauled the remains to asheries. John Henne and his wife chose a unique trade—they established a small willow ranch on the bottom land in Sheboygan, and from the willow twigs they fashioned a variety of baskets.

Stimulating the growth of the city was immigration, which reached its peak during the 1850s. In 1854, according to Michael Lynch, then the deputy collector for Sheboygan, 20,914 people disembarked at the port. In 1855 they numbered 65,381. Hotels were built to accommodate the crush, and livery stables and cartage companies were begun to transport and move the crowds. Most of the hotels that lined Pennsylvania Avenue and Center Street were really taverns with a few rooms for lodging. In 1850 there were 11 of these establishments, among them the Green Mountain House, Warren

This 1867 bird's-eye view of Sheboygan shows the city clustered around the harbor and river with many sailing vessels near the port. The point of land jutting into the lake in the upper right hand corner is "North Point" site of the light-house.

House, Merchants' Hotel, Brown's Temperance House, and the Sheboygan House.

Although Sheboygan had a good natural harbor to receive the many ships that landed there, a finger of land caused the river to make a sharp turn to the north before it entered Lake Michigan near the foot of Center Avenue. If this small bar of land could be cut through, ships would have a more direct access to the port.

In January 1852 a public meeting was called with delegates from every town attending to discuss the harbor. Silas Stedman was elected president of the convention, which included William Farnsworth, Charles Cole, A.P. Lyman, Harrison Hobart, and other prominent men in the county. The state legislature approved the action and authorized the committee to borrow funds to finance the project. A dredge was purchased to cut through the land and straighten the harbor entrance. The dredged land was used to fill the original channel.

This finger of land was known as Kirkland's Point for its owner, Joseph Kirkland, one of Sheboygan's most enterprising promoters who aided virtually every transaction of the young community. Owner of the south pier and its warehouses, he also was president of the village in 1847, director of the Bank of Sheboygan, shipowner, commissioner of the Sheboygan and Mississippi Railroad, and later a stockholder in the Sheboygan and Fond du Lac Railroad.

Kirkland lived in a mansion located on a bank called Kirkland's Bluff south of the harbor. In the spring of 1852 a fierce gale swept away both the north and south piers. When the harbor entrance was dredged, resulting in the relocation of the harbor entrance to Pennsylvania Avenue, and the piers rebuilt, wave action eroded the clay bank upon which his house was built. It eventually slid into the lake.

Kirkland was instrumental in attempts to build the first railroad in the county. As the leading grain and commission merchant, he foresaw the importance of the railway, not only to himself but to the whole county. In 1852 he acquired the franchises and privileges of the plans drawn up by a group in 1847. There was much opposition and behind-the-scenes politics before the first track was laid in 1856. Kirkland's investment in the project, over $20,000, resulted in the foreclosure of much of his property in 1857. The railroad never did make any money for its first investors, and by 1860 track had only been laid as far as Glenbeulah, a distance of 20 miles.

Kirkland became the president of the Sheboygan and Mississippi Railroad in 1856. While president he had track laid so that freight cars could enter his warehouse to pick up goods. The *Evergreen City Times* of June 28, 1856, congratulated him on his "good fortune in having the freight depot so near his warehouse and pier."

Betsy Oakley Wade, wife of Sylvanus Wade, pioneered in Greenbush, Wisconsin, and helped to make the Wade House a special stop on the Fond du Lac Plank Road. The Wade House remained in the family's possession until 1941. Courtesy, Old Wade House Collection

FARMERS AND FISHERMEN

Farming in the county before the 1850s was a small-scale family affair. After clearing the land and getting in a crop, the farmer only raised enough food for his family with little excess to trade or barter. Maple trees were tapped for their syrup; cheese and butter making were done by the housewife to supply the needs of her family. The first crop planted was usually corn, as it could be grown between the roots and stumps of the trees. Agriculture lagged in the county until enough land could be cleared to produce in excess of the family's needs. Of course, there were few markets for farm produce and they were difficult to reach.

Corn soon was replaced by wheat as the major crop. Many of the settlers from New England were wheat farmers who knew that grain was easy to produce on the newly cleared land. For 30 years, from 1850 to 1880, the county led in the state's production of wheat, which was of such fine quality that it gained a reputation in the principal markets of the country and enjoyed the distinction of a special quotation in Milwaukee, Chicago, Buffalo, and New York.

With more and more wheat to export and immigration reaching its peak, Sheboygan became one of the most prominent distributing ports in the state. The *Evergreen City Times* of June 23, 1855, stated:

The teeming business between this city and Fond du Lac is enormous. Our streets in the vicinity of the piers and warehouses are almost continually a literal blockade. Every team coming in with

Facing page: Gilbert Smith built this home for his family in 1874 on a bluff overlooking Lake Michigan. Complete with widow's walk so that his family could watch his fishing boats come to port, the house was built in the old village of Amsterdam, in the town of Holland. Time has erased the village but the home still stands. Courtesy, Sheboygan County Landmarks, LTD.

grain, or loading out with goods, is registered at the warehouse on its arrival, and must take its turn in discharging and loading, and often times is compeled to wait 12-48 hours before its turn comes. There are now between 400 and 500 teams engaged on this route, and produce accumulates here faster than vessels can be found to take it away.

Fishing, one of the first industries to be established, was also a major business. Fishermen from Ohio, where the fishing grounds of Lake Erie were becoming depleted, spent the summer months fishing along the lakeshore and returned home in the fall when the stormy weather set in.

One fisherman from Ohio who decided to stay in the county was David Wilson. He settled along the lakeshore in the town of Wilson (named for him) in 1840 and brought his family there two years later. In 1845 he was joined by the Osgood brothers, James and Leonard, and the following year by Joseph Fairchild. All of these men made their living by fishing.

The town of Holland became the home of Gilbert Smith in 1847. He established a fishing business and platted the village of Amsterdam in 1852. Considered to be the wealthiest man in the township, he also operated a lumberyard and a general storage business dealing in fish, feed, salt, and other products. His sons began the Smith Brothers Fish Company and the famous restaurant in Port Washington, Wisconsin.

THE CIVIL WAR AND ITS AFTERMATH

Sheboygan's commerce was geared entirely to lake traffic during the 1850s. Little thought was given to what the construction of the railroad lines might do to Great Lakes shipping. Nor did the people of Sheboygan, so far removed from the nation's capital, pay much attention to the talk of secession in the South, until the news of the fall of Fort Sumter reached Sheboygan County on Sunday, April 14, 1861. Milwaukee newspapers brought in by steamer that morning bore the startling headlines. Printers at the *Evergreen City Times* were called in to set type for an "extra" edition that was sent by couriers throughout the county to spread the news.

A German militia company, fully armed and trained, was stationed in Sheboygan. Wisconsin's Governor Randall telegraphed the militia leader, Captain Friederich Aude, that there was a chance for his company to volunteer as a body but in lieu of volunteering for duty his company should ship its arms to Madison. The captain

called the militia together, they met, stacked their arms, and declined to serve.

A Mr. (later General) Sweet was instructed to gather the guns and send them to Madison if the men failed to enlist. Upon hearing that the militia had declined the enlistment and that Sweet was after their arms, Charles T. Moore, a Sheboygan merchant, replied that if the governor wanted the guns he need not send anyone for them. There were enough men willing and ready to take them to him!

Moore and a few men sought out Solomon Coon, who could beat a drum, and Addison Manville, who played the fife. Commandeering a dray, they followed Coon and Manville to the armory to demand the guns. With drum beating and fife shrilling, the procession broke up the Reverend Camp's meeting at the Congregational church and added the parishioners to their impromptu parade. The guns were willingly given up and the citizens took them to the drugstore, where they were stacked and guarded.

With the guns secured, Moore drove to Sheboygan Falls to see if a company could be formed for service and save the city from the disgrace of sending those arms to Madison without the men to use them. Arriving at the Falls, Moore appealed to James and Nathan Cole to assist in saving the good name of the county and to organize a company to take the deserted guns to the front. The Cole brothers told him to go back to Sheboygan, assuring him that enough men from the Falls would go that very day to make up the company.

The young men thought about calling out the brass band, but it being the Sabbath they only took a fife and a large drum. The Baptist church, where Deacon William Trowbridge was preaching, was the first to be disturbed by the noise. The congregation walked out of church to be confronted by the deacon's grandsons, along with several other young men making a rather unholy din. When apprised of the news, the deacon took the drum from Nathan and strapped it on himself. Word quickly spread that Deacon Trowbridge, who had strong views about keeping the Sabbath, was beating a drum on Sunday, and within a short time the whole village turned out to hear the fateful news.

The Stedman Guards were formed that day, with Nathan Cole the first man in the county to sign the enlistment roll. Only 18, he became the youngest man in the Fourth Wisconsin Regiment. He served 18 months and then came home for recruits, returning to the battlefields shortly thereafter with about 50 men. Wounded at the Battle of Prairie Grove, he continued to serve his country until resigning his commission as major in June 1867.

Meetings were held throughout the county to urge the enlistment of volunteers. By the following Sunday the first company was organized under Captain Edmund B. Gray, principal of Sheboygan's Union High School. It became Company C, Fourth Wisconsin Volunteer Infantry, and later was reorganized as a cavalry regiment. The company left Sheboygan on June 16, 1861, on the steamer *Comet* bound for Racine. The unit saw its first action on June 28 when it was ordered to Milwaukee to aid in quelling the bank riots. Warren Reed of the town of Lyndon, shot during the disturbance, became the first Sheboygan County fatality. On July 15 the regiment was ordered into active duty at Baltimore.

Gustavus Wintermeyer was a student in the law office of J.A. Bentley of Sheboygan when the Civil War began. He promptly volunteered as a private in Company C, 4th Regiment for the Wisconsin Volunteers. Rising rapidly in rank, he was named adjutant of the regiment in May 1863 and took part in the bloody assaults on Port Hudson, Louisiana, where he was among the 220 men who lived to return to their line of duty. Courtesy, Sheboygan County Museum Collection

A German company called the Sheboygan Tigers was organized in September 1861. The *National Demokrat* of September 25, 1861, said:

The Sheboygan Tigers left us yesterday amid the roll of the drum, music and the thunder of cannon ... An immense crowd of citizens accompanied them to the boat where they bade farewell to their dear ones.

Other companies raised in the county about the same time were the Freemont Rangers at Cascade, the Forest Union Rifles in the western part of the county, and an Irish company called the Concoran Guards. Eight more companies would follow during the next three years as a total of 2,215 Sheboygan County soldiers went to war. Only 479 were drafted; the rest volunteered. Nearly 300 never returned.

Many of these men were foreign-born or born in the United States to immigrant parents. But here, as in other parts of the country, they showed their love for America by volunteering to fight and by being in the forefront of battle.

There was excitement on the home front, too. On September 3, 1862, an Indian scare created wholesale panic in the county. According to the *Evergreen City Times*, a solitary rider pulled up in front of the Kossuth House, "almost speechless with excitement and fright," and uttered the dreaded word:

. . . Ingins! Ingins! Ingins! The red devils, fifty strong, were burning Centerville, twelve miles north on the lake shore, and massacring all the inhabitants! And every man and boy that could shoulder a musket or carry a pitchfork was frantically called upon to fly at once to the rescue.

As the day advanced, further "witnesses" arrived in Sheboygan, each compounding the number of Indians and their crimes. By noon they were claiming that 300 Indians, each equipped with new U.S. rifles, were on the warpath. The roads were lined with wagon loads of families streaming into the city for protection. It was estimated that more than 4,000 people had crowded into Sheboygan by nightfall.

It was the same story throughout the county. Farmers left their tools standing in the fields with fences open so that the cattle and horses roamed at will over the countryside. As night approached, people hid in cornfields or gathered together in the stoutest houses guarded by pitchforks and axes. The Indian scare spread to the north and south as far as Port Washington and Milwaukee, where the citizens called Governor Salomon to order out the Light Infantry to save the city.

With the dawn of the next day, sheepish residents slowly made their way back to their homes. Not an Indian had been seen during the entire time, and riders sent out as scouts could only report that everything was normal.

A Milwaukee editor, writing about the incident later, said:

The human family is at times ridiculous or frightened or desperate or foolish or cowardly, but never until the Indian scare of 1862 were the dwellers of Milwaukee and Wisconsin possessed of all five of these attributes at once.

Another interesting sidelight to the Civil War years in the county was the residency of Captain Jonathan Walker, the famed abolitionist who was immortalized by John Greenleaf Whittier's poem "The Man with the Branded Hand." Walker, his abolitionist work finished, moved to Sheboygan County in 1852 with his wife and the youngest of their 10 children. They settled on a small farm near the village of Winooski and lived there until they moved to Muskegon, Michigan, in 1863. The farm was rumored to have been a way station on the underground railroad, but it never has been proven.

Slowly the war years rolled on. The list of battles in which Sheboygan County men fought read like a litany of the Civil War: Shiloh,

Jonathan Walker, pictured here in 1844, was described in a family history as a sailor, father, adventurer, and abolitionist. He moved to Sheboygan County in 1852 and allegedly conducted an underground railroad from the town of Mitchell. Courtesy, Elmer R. Koppelmann

Pictured here is one of the antislavery pamphlets written and distributed by Captain Jonathan Walker, the Man with the Branded Hand. Courtesy, Elmer R. Koppelmann

Corinth, Perryville, Fayetteville, Port Hudson, Vicksburg, Helena, Chickamauga, Look Out Mountain, and Sherman's march to the sea.

But the war did end and the men returned home. They came back in small groups or by the wagon load. They were older, thinner, wiser, and had memories that would fade only with time. These were not the same young men who had marched off to battle amidst the cheers of their fellow citizens. Most were ready to slip into their former lives, but others, restless after seeing more of their country than they had ever dreamed possible, were ready to move on to new places: Iowa, Minnesota, the Dakotas, and California. Many families packed up their belongings and traveled north and west to begin new lives in these states.

The great majority, of course, remained in the county. General Konrad Krez took a little time off and then ran for his old job as district attorney. He held the office for six years before retiring into private practice and later moving to Milwaukee. General Harrison Hobart also moved to Milwaukee and ran for governor of Wisconsin four times without ever winning the office. He was elected to the legislature, however, and served with distinction. Captain Carlos Mansfield was urged to become a justice of the peace again but declined the offer, content to remain on his Greenbush farm.

Dr. Adolph St. Sure and his son George, also a doctor, returned to Sheboygan to resume their practices, as did Dr. John L. Shepard and Sheboygan's two Civil War nurses, Helen Brainard Cole and Emily Watson Chamberlain Squire. Major Nathan Cole, the last to return, was elected register of deeds and eventually became deputy collector of internal revenue and postmaster of the City of Sheboygan.

One who did not return was Adjutant Gustavus Wintermeyer. Killed at the Battle of Port Hudson, Wintermeyer was not forgotten. Twenty years later, when Sheboygan's Grand Army of the Republic post was organized, it was named Gustavus Wintermeyer Post Number 187.

Chapter III

CHAIRS, CHEESE, AND CHILDREN

Between 1860 and 1880 Sheboygan grew the least, was the poorest, most poverty-stricken, dilapidated city in Wisconsin. Able-bodied men worked ten hours a day on the public streets for the city at sixty cents a day, and as there was no money in the city treasury, they were glad to get store-pay from the city treasurer.

In a speech to manufacturers, Thomas Blackstock, president of the Phoenix Chair Company, introduced himself as the man from the city of three "C's": chairs, cheese, and children. It was a catchy phrase, and Sheboyganites adopted it as their slogan. Later a fourth "C" was added: churches. Courtesy, Sheboygan County Historical Research Center

Sheboygan was thus described by Thomas M. Blackstock, president of the Phoenix Chair Company, in a speech to local manufacturers in 1904.

After a quarter century of steady increases, Sheboygan County's growth rate slowed after the Civil War. In 1860 the county had a population of 27,082 living in 5,469 homes. The number of improved acres of land totaled 107,245. By 1870 the population had

Above: In Sheboygan County, the first monument to soldiers of the Civil War was erected by citizens in the town of Rhine in July 1868. Of the 115 young men who joined the Union Army from the township, 23 never returned. Their names are carved into the base of the marble shaft along with the places they fell: Chancellorsville, Chaplin Hills, and Gettysburg. The eagle that tops the monument is a replica of "Old Abe," the bald eagle mascot of the 8th Regiment of Wisconsin Volunteers. Photo by Fred Horneck

increased to only 31,759 in 5,738 homes. Improved land, however, totaled 150,093 acres.

Many factors contributed to this condition. Railroads had taken over much of the transportation business from the sailing vessels, an adaptation that shipping-conscious Sheboygan County was slow to make. The Civil War took its toll of young men, and economic conditions after the war were generally depressed.

"CHAIR CITY"

But all was not gloomy. The 20 years between 1865 and 1885 saw the beginnings of the furniture industry in Sheboygan, which would lead to its appellation as "Chair City." An early chair, a small, rather crude model, was given to the Sheboygan County Museum by descendants of Darius Leavens of Sheboygan Falls. It seems that the Jonathan Leighton family was expecting relatives from the East, and not having any chairs to sit upon, they hired Leavens to build several for the expected guests.

The first factory established for the manufacture of furniture was begun in 1865 by Silas Crocker and L.E. Minott. The factory had once been the site of the American House, a pretentious brick and frame hotel built by Louis C. Gury in the mid-1850s. The three-story hotel was topped by an observatory and crowned by a dome. A flagpole mounted on the dome flew the flag daily, and on the Fourth of July, Gury, with patriotic fervor, would throw open the dining rooms and feed everyone who showed up. His largess and the depressed times of the 1860s caused Gury to suffer financial reverses, and he committed suicide.

The hotel stood empty for several years until Minott and Crocker purchased the building and converted it into a furniture factory. The two men acquired the steam engine and fixtures of the Union Steam Flouring Mills of Glenbeulah, which was being dismantled, and were in business. They conducted a saw and planing mill and manufactured chairs and cabinetwork. Minott later sold his share to a Mr. Bliss, and the firm was known as Crocker and Bliss until it was destroyed by fire in April 1875.

Another early chair company began as the Morse Bending Company, an ox yoke manufacturer that incorporated in 1869 as the Sheboygan Manufacturing Company. Twenty-five employees turned out 1,200 bent stock chairs per day. In 1883 the business was destroyed by fire. The investors immediately reorganized and rebuilt, naming it the Sheboygan Chair Company. The firm was successfully run by local interests until 1942, when a Philadelphia concern purchased the business. In 1952 they sold the three main divisions of the company to three different owners.

Sheboygan welcomed the Grand Army of the Republic (G.A.R.) state convention in June 1925 with parades, banquets, and speeches. Seen here are veterans in front of the Civil War monument in Fountain Park. From left to right, standing: A.J. Calkins, S.S. Chandler, Peter Klein, B. Schemmer, George Breed, A.S. Eaton, Peter Lenhardt, Frank Dagle, C.V. Clark, and J.F. Minch. Seated: N. McCollam, Lawrence Miller, Robert Law, Phad Sheerin, W.W. Hubbard, and Thomas Reeds. Photo by Sheboygan Press

The Crocker Chair Company was incorporated in 1880 and was one of the largest chair factories in the country. It produced cane and wood upholstered chairs for 40 years. The company, however, went bankrupt in 1932, and the buildngs were razed in that year. Courtesy, Sheboygan County Historical Research Center

Before the establishment of these two firms, several retail furniture stores were selling hand-made chairs constructed on the premises. They were Christian Albrecht, Ernst Arens, Christian Riedel, Frederick Walther, and Herman Wolters. All of these stores were located on Eighth Street, which was becoming a street of shops and businesses.

The burning of the Crocker and Bliss Company was a severe blow to the city, putting many men out of work. Thomas Blackstock, one of Sheboygan's leading citizens and community builders, organized the Phoenix Chair Company in May 1875. He was the principal stockholder and president of the company for many years. Initially the chair company employed 75 men and had a capital stock of $50,000. By 1888 the firm employed 400 to 500 hands and had a capital stock of $300,000. Situated on 15 acres of land, it became one of the largest chair factories in the world.

During the 1930s Depression, the firm almost went bankrupt but was restructured and survived. A part of the Sheboygan Chair Company was purchased in 1952 and combined with the Phoenix, then sold to Milwaukee investors in December 1957. In 1962 the company suffered a $362,000 arson fire, and in April 1963 the president of the firm, Marlin Weisse, was killed in a traffic accident. Unable to sustain these losses, the company was closed in January 1964 and the assets sold at auction. In 1967 Ebenreiter Lumber Company purchased the buildings, which were razed in 1980.

In 1873 Edgar A. Hill built a frame factory for the manufacture of baby carriages, doll carts, wagons, hobby horses, and other toys. It was not a successful business and Hill sold it to the Sheboygan Carriage Company in 1876. The carriage company was sold in 1880 to the Crockers, whose chair factory had burned in 1875. The Crocker Chair Company would be one of the largest employers in Sheboygan for the next 40 years. The company was reorganized in 1924, when Dr. G.W. Brickbauer purchased the controlling interest, but was closed during the Depression. In 1932 the T-shaped, four-story building was razed. During those hard times residents were encouraged to take all of the lumber, except the beams, for fuel.

Another famous chair factory was the Mattoon Manufacturing Company. George Mattoon came to Sheboygan Falls in 1865 to work for his brother Obed, who had started a chair factory and store. After three years Obed sold his furniture store to George, who expanded the business to Plymouth and Sheboygan. In 1881 the two brothers leased a part of the Freyberg Flour and Grist Mill in Sheboygan and started a table factory.

In 1883 George Mattoon purchased a site on the west side of the river, which was then a swamp, and constructed a three-story factory. Beginning with 35 employees, the business grew to eventually employ over 1,000. In 1886 the firm was incorporated. A fire in 1888 destroyed the plant but a larger one was built. By 1892 the Mattoon Company was supplying electric power to the city of Sheboygan. George Mattoon died in 1904 and the company's name was changed to Northern Chair Company. Members of the Reiss family purchased the company in 1916. In his autobiography published in 1937, Jacob L. Reiss stated:

In 1916 the Bank of Sheboygan had among its assets the Northern Furniture Co., an old concern I had looked up to as a boy, as one of the greatest industries of the town . . .

The bank tried to dispose of it but couldn't find a buyer. My brother Peter, a staunch Sheboyganite, was very much upset about the possibility of this factory closing down and remarked that it was going to be a great blow to the community for it would throw 800 people out of work with little hope of finding re-employment. It was a sentimental case of the home-town boy coming to the rescue and together with my brothers, we formed a company with a capital of $700,000.

Following Peter's death in 1927, Jacob Reiss moved to Sheboygan with his son Raymond to assume management of the firm. In 1962 the firm was sold to Franklin Industries, a division of United

Above: Sheboygan was not the only community in the county to manufacture chairs. This advertisement for Plymouth Rockers was included in the Plymouth Chair Company catalogue. Courtesy, Sheboygan County Historical Research Center

Right: The freighter Helena *was the largest vessel built in Sheboygan. Launched from the Rieboldt & Wolters Shipyard in the summer of 1887, all factories closed so everyone could attend the celebration. Two years later the* Helena *sank after colliding with another boat. From the launching of the first ship, the* Pilot, *in 1845, until the closing of the Rieboldt & Wolters Shipyard in 1896, Sheboygan's shipyards were an important asset and employed hundreds of men. Courtesy,* Sheboygan Press

Industrial Syndicate of New York. Thomas J. Reiss, Jr., Jacob's great-grandson, announced the purchase of R Way in July 1987, bringing ownership of the company back into the family once again.

The American Manufacturing Company, which began as a toy manufacturer in 1887, turned to making cane and maple chairs and in 1909 introduced a fiber furniture line. In 1916 the name was changed to the American Chair Company. It was sold in 1924 to outside interests and in 1941 to the Thonet Company. The name was changed to Thonet in 1969. The plant, which covered an entire city block, was destroyed in an explosion and fire in April 1982. The site was cleared and the company did not rebuild.

The Madewell Chair Company was founded in 1917 by a group of men headed by Silas H. Crocker, a member of the family who established the Crocker Chair Company. The company made fiber furniture until 1937, when rockers and upholstered sofas and chairs were manufactured. Over 1,000 men were employed at the peak of its business. In 1972 the company was sold to William Forbes, who began to market custom-made furniture in the 1980s through his Cobblepeg Shops.

Many other furniture factories were begun in Sheboygan and in the county. These included the Valley Furniture Company, 1925; McNeill Chair Company, 1915; Art Furniture Company, 1904; Northfield Company, 1905; and Western Furniture, 1910.

Why did Sheboygan industries turn to the manufacture of chairs and furniture with such success? With sawmills on the rivers and the abundance of cut timber, lumber was plentiful and relatively cheap. The demand for furniture in the area was high, as the arduous journey to the county precluded bringing along much in the way of household furnishings. In addition, Sheboygan's shipyards attracted ships' carpenters, sail makers, and other craftsmen who also turned their hand to furniture making. Ship captains and crews who wintered in Sheboygan were on hand to handle the factories' cargo with the commencement of shipping in the spring. The resumption of the flow of immigrants to the area in the 1880s brought skilled workers to Sheboygan—carpenters, cabinetmakers, woodworkers, and artisans of all sorts, many of whom worked in the furniture factories. During the 1880s Sheboygan experienced a boom period that would last until World War I.

SHEBOYGAN BECOMES THE "BIG CHEESE"

The art of cheese making was brought to the county by the Yankee settlers. The first cheeses were made from excess milk cooked in kettles hung over the kitchen fire. There was no science and little skill connected to this method.

Commercial cheese making began in the county shortly after the arrival of the Smith family, who were familiar with the cheese industry in their native New York. Two of the brothers, Hiram and John, began making cheese in 1858. Each of them owned about a dozen cows (the largest herds in the county); John gathered curd from neighboring farms and pressed it, together with their own, into cheese. This method was known as the "Ohio plan."

In the fall of that year, John barreled 58 cheese and took them to Chicago to sell. Dealers were not interested in Wisconsin cheese, wanting only the New York product. In desperation John paid a dealer one dollar to inspect the cheese. The result was the purchase of all the cheese for eight cents a pound.

This method of cheese making was only partially successful. The cheese was often inferior and lacked uniformity. Farmers left so much whey in the curd that it drove the profit out of the venture. John Smith abandoned the project to his brother Hiram, who was soon joined by Ira Strong. In 1861 they began collecting milk rather than curd from their neighbors, thus maintaining control over the process.

Hiram Conover, a brother-in-law of Smith's, began making cheese shortly after the Civil War. In his new woodshed on his farm he installed a cheese vat purchased in New York. Conover sent his son Seth to New York to learn scientific cheese making. He later built a cheese factory in Plymouth, which became one of the largest and most successful in the county.

In 1864 Ambrose DeLand started collecting milk and making cheese in the town of Lima, installing cheese-making equipment in his new barn in 1865. DeLand kept a herd of 50 cows in summer and 40 in winter. In later years he increased his herd to more than 100. DeLand manufactured cheese for 27 years and won more premiums than any cheese maker in the state. In 1876 he was awarded a bronze medal at the Centennial Exposition in Philadelphia for a giant cheese of 300 pounds. The cheese was pressed in a cider press and banded by hoops made out of staves cut from his own woods.

The first cheese factory in the county independent of other farm buildings and built for that express purpose was erected for Manning McKinnon in 1867. By 1871 there were 20 cheese factories in the county. They operated four to eight months of the year, producing 500,000 pounds of cheese at an average price of 10 to 12 cents per pound.

In 1872 the first cheese factory in the town of Rhine was begun by Katherine Feldman, whose husband Helwig owned 650 acres of not very fertile land. She traveled to New York to learn the art of cheese making, accomplishing the task in six weeks and becoming the first woman cheese maker in the county. A letter to her grand-daughter in 1940 from her helper, Phillip Kasper, reads in part:

On August 8, 1884, I started to work for your grandmother. Your Uncle Mike Feldman came after me close to midnight August 7. We were all in bed after putting in three or four extra hours in the harvest field, binding and shocking the last of the oats, and we were ready to start hauling in the grain the next day.

We were not in bed very long before someone rapped at the door and my father got up and it was your Uncle Michael as they call him in German. My father didn't know what he wanted at that late hour of the night. "My mother sent me over here to get Phillip to help her make cheese tomorrow."

"Why, I can't let him go; we have all our grain out in the field and have all arrangements made to haul the grain in tomorrow. I'll send one of the men over to help you." But my dad was not very anxious to let me go and he said, "I'll send two men over to help your mother."

Farmers brought their milk to the Ourtown cheese factory and the daily gathering gave them an opportunity to exchange views on crops and the weather. Fred Boldt was the cheesemaker when this photo was taken in 1892. Courtesy, Sheboygan County Historical Research Center

A typical country cheese factory was run by Ed Wunsch in Sheboygan County. In 1944 there were 65 of these factories in the county. Sheboygan County Historical Research Center

But Michael said his mother told him not to come without Phillip. Even though tired from a long day's work I was anxious to go. Their farm and cheese factory was just one mile south from my home across the field . . . It was the longest mile I ever walked in all my life, for I was so tired.

From the very first morning I was treated with the same kindness as if a member of the family, and it was only a few days before I went along with the work the same as if born and raised in the family and worked with her for years . . . She never had to drive me; I knew what there was to do and did it . . . from 4 P.M. until night. I was only there ten days when I was left alone one day and made fine cheese.

Your grandmother was far beyond the average person in intelligence—after helping her husband to work on that large farm out in the wilderness she then established the first cheese factory in the town of Rhine.

Why your grandmother chose me as a helper, for she had only seen me a few times and there were dozens of boys in the neighborhood to choose from, I don't know. There was prosperity on that farm—40 cows to milk morning and night. Even though your uncle was taking care of the farm, your grandmother was the manager, and her advice was always sought.

When cheese making was begun in the county, farmers had

only scrub cows and hogs, oxen, and small horses. They were impoverishing the land by raising unrotated wheat on the same fields year after year. This mismanagement, coupled with the devastation from the chinch bug and army worm, brought an end to large-scale wheat farming. A new age of agriculture was beginning.

Improvements in farming were aided by the formation of agricultural societies. In 1851 the first of these, the Sheboygan County Agricultural Society, was formed. The society held its first exhibition that year in Sheboygan Falls. It was followed by the Sheboygan County Farmers Club in 1859.

In 1867 the German Agricultural and Traders Society was begun. Tired of being unrecognized for their superior talents in farming, the German farmers banded together to run their own agricultural fair. Year after year the Agricultural Society had spurned their best produce, awarding fair premiums to Yankee farmers. Know-nothingism, which was at its height in the county during the 1860s, contributed to this hostility toward foreigners, an attitude that was not overcome until the turn of the century.

Yankees looked down on the settlers from continental Europe, particularly Germans, and ignorantly referred to them as "Dutchmen." This social attitude, born of ignorance and prejudice, left a lasting memory with Alfred Marschner, a young German boy living in Sheboygan. He was invited to the home of a Yankee friend for an after-school treat. The mother gave an apple to her son, but there was none for the little "Dutchman." Years later Marschner, a pioneer German newspaper editor and avid historian of the county, would recall the incident with sorrow.

The fledgling dairy industry of the county would reap the most benefit from the agricultural societies and the stocking of blooded livestock. For years, livestock had been allowed to wander at will and forage for themselves, resulting in half-starved cattle that produced milk of dubious flavor. The penning of cattle, the provision for shelter during inclement weather, and the introduction of rich tame grasses on the farms was begun when the farmer realized the value of providing for his animals.

As the dairy industry grew and prospered, new marketing methods were introduced. Professional buyers who traveled to factories to purchase the output of cheese makers felt they were losing profits and soon organized dairy boards of trade. These boards, the first of which was organized at Sheboygan Falls on May 22, 1873, were able to equalize prices through competitive biddings. As the quality of Wisconsin cheese became recognized, outside wholesale and commission houses maintained permanent agents in the county, and local firms of dealers also were started. In 1913 Henry Krumrey of

Mission House College was organized in 1862 as a Christian Institution of Higher Education operated by the Evangelical and Reformed Church. As the college grew, it attracted more than students of the ministry, and coeducation was introduced in 1931. In 1956 the seminary and college were separated and the name changed to Lakeland College. Lakeland celebrated its 125th anniversary in 1987. Courtesy, Lakeland College Collection

Plymouth introduced a cooperative marketing association. At its peak the federation had a membership of 435 cheese factories and handled one-tenth of the American cheese made in Wisconsin.

Known as the "Cheese Capital of the World," Plymouth became the center of the cheese industry in the county. Sales of Plymouth cheeses affected cheese prices all over the country. During World War II the government purchased almost all of the cheese offered on the exchange. Today the cheese industry is still centralized in Plymouth, where some of the biggest names of the industry—Sargento, S&R, Borden, Kraft, and Tolibia—are located.

SHEBOYGAN SCHOOL DAYS

The county's educational system was begun along with the settlement of the county. The first school, taught during the winter of 1836-1837 by F.M. Rublee in Sheboygan, was short-lived, and the settlement was abandoned. Children were then taught in private homes, but as the population increased the demand for schools increased. The town of Sheboygan established the first school district in 1840. This district's school, located near Farnsworth's Mill, was not strictly a public school. Residents who sent their children there paid half of the operating expenses, and nonresidents had to pay tuition. The second school district was established at Sheboygan Falls. Two parochial schools—Trinity Lutheran and St. Mary Magdalen (now Holy Name)—were begun in 1852. These early schools had two terms, winter and summer. Older children usually attended the winter term and worked during the summer session.

The large German population presented an educational prob-

The Union School was opened for classes on October 20, 1856. The school was free to all within the city limits, and there were three departments: primary, intermediate, and high school. The school served Sheboygan's children for 112 years, a state record. The old building was razed in 1969. Courtesy, Sheboygan Press

lem. One-half of the children attending district schools in 1872 spoke only German. Proud of their language and heritage, the German parents believed strongly that their children should be taught in German. The subject became a burning issue of the time and parochial schools, which were taught in German, flourished. In time, however, English became the common language, and the demand for teaching in German gradually disappeared.

With the settlement of hundreds of Hmong families in Sheboygan after the Vietnam War, English as a second language has become an issue again. In time, it, too, undoubtedly will be resolved in much the same way.

Higher education has always been important to county residents. In 1853 the Sheboygan Academy was opened. Taught by local people, the academy flourished until the death of its president, Fordyce Williams, when it gradually faded away. In 1859 a Catholic college was built by St. Mary Magdalen Church with the intention of its becoming a girls' school, but it, too, faded out of existence.

Mission House College was begun near Franklin in the late 1850s. The Lippers, the sponsors of the college, donated the land upon which it was built. After their immigration to the county, the Lippers petitioned the Reformed churches in Germany to send ministers, but were advised to educate and train their own. In 1855 they began the education of students in the town of Herman, which had no schools. Students were given instructions by the Immanuel and Saron congregations.

The first building at the college was completed in 1864.

Children loved to visit Fountain Park in the heart of downtown Sheboygan. The block square park was set aside as a public square when the village was first platted in 1836 and remains a park today. An artesian well was dug there in 1875 and provided water to the fountain as well as water for firefighting. Although the high mineral content of the water corroded the piping, rendering it unfit for firefighting, a small drinking fountain remains a feature of the park today. Courtesy, Sheboygan Press

Education was free to any student who wished to join the ministry, but the young men were asked to sign an agreement that if they failed to join, they would pay the school $100 for each year of their instruction.

The college grew slowly but steadily. By 1940 the enrollment had grown to 200 students, who were offered a course of study comparable to any other small college of the time. In 1949 the faculties of the college and seminary were segregated, and in 1956 the college and seminary themselves were separated. The Sheboygan Business College was purchased from its president, Emil C. Muuss, in 1954, and the school of business was moved to the campus in 1956. When the name of the college was changed to Lakeland, the mission was no longer limited to educating only ministers. In 1987 Lakeland celebrated its 125th anniversary. Today the coed college offers a full range of credits in its park-like setting.

In 1920 the Sheboygan County Normal School, for the education of students wanting to become teachers, was begun in rooms above Bade's Drug Store in Plymouth. Organized by two local teachers, Flita Luedke and Nellie Thomas, the Normal School moved to new quarters built in Sheboygan Falls in 1924. During the Depression of the 1930s, the teacher-training course was expanded from a one-year term to two years. The Sheboygan County school was one of the last normal schools to be phased out by the State of Wisconsin in the 1960s. In 1968 it became a school for special education and the handicapped. The name was changed in 1975 to Lightfoot School in honor of Ray B. Lightfoot, who served the county's education needs for 42 years, 25 as superintendent of schools.

Two other schools offer post-high school training: the Lakeshore Technical Institute in Cleveland, Manitowoc County, and the University of Wisconsin-Sheboygan campus. The vocational and technical school, long housed in old buildings in Sheboygan and Manitowoc, moved to a $5-million, 160-acre campus in 1974. The school functions day and night yearlong to accommodate students attending full-or part-time instruction.

The University of Wisconsin-Sheboygan, part of the county since 1933, was housed by the vocational school and staffed by traveling professors from the Extension Division until the mid-1960s. The need for a campus and resident professors was met in 1964 when the beautiful Center was opened on the west side of Sheboygan.

Offering a two-year associate degree, the Center prepares students to finish their education at the university in Madison or at other state or private institutions.

Chapter IV

THE KOHLER-VOLLRATH DYNASTY

Walter J. Kohler, wearing the straw hat, crosses the picket line set up in front of the company's offices on July 16, 1934. Although the company reopened in September 1934, the controversy was not officially settled until seven years later. In May 1941 an agreement was signed between the Kohler Company and the American Federation of Labor. Courtesy, Sheboygan Press

The Kohler name has become almost synonymous with Sheboygan County during this century. The brand name "Kohler of Kohler" graces bathroom fixtures in mansions and cottages, government and private buildings, and luxury hotels and diners in the United States and abroad. Known for high quality of workmanship and originality of color and design, "Kohler of Kohler" fixtures are eagerly sought after and have made the Kohler Company the largest manufacturer of plumbing ware in the world. Today the nearly billion-dollar firm is headed by Herbert V. Kohler, Jr., grandson of John Michael Kohler, founder of the company.

Several of John Michael Kohler's descendants head some of the most prestigious firms in the county. Ruth De Young Kohler, Her-

Jacob J. Vollrath, a German immigrant, founded the Vollrath Company in Sheboygan, Wisconsin, in 1874. Today his great-great-grandson, Terry Kohler, heads the giant firm which bears the family's name. Courtesy, Vollrath Company

bert's sister and the only granddaughter of John Michael, is the director of the John Michael Kohler Arts Center in Sheboygan. A great-grandson, Terry Kohler, is chairman and chief executive officer of the Vollrath Company of Sheboygan, while two other great-grandsons, brothers Walter III and Peter Kohler, head the Kohler-General Company of Sheboygan Falls.

AN AMERICAN SUCCESS STORY

The story of the Kohler family begins with two men, John Michael Kohler and Jacob J. Vollrath.

Jacob Vollrath was born in Dorrebach, Germany, in 1824. His father died when he was two years old and his mother married Johann Meyer in 1828. At the age of 19, having completed his apprenticeship as an iron moulder, Jacob was drafted by the Prussian army. His stepfather was able to secure an exemption for him and Jacob made plans to follow his aunt and uncle, Susanna and Philipp Weimer, to the United States.

In the spring of 1844, he crossed the border into Belgium and secured passage aboard a British sailing vessel. He was followed to Albany, New York, where he settled near the Weimers, by his mother, stepfather, and their three children in 1846. Plans were already in progress to move to Wisconsin via the Erie Canal, which had just opened to travel.

The two families settled in Rockfield, about 20 miles northwest of Milwaukee, but Jacob, who had no skills as a farmer, returned to Milwaukee to find employment. There he met Elisabetha Fuchs, who had immigrated from Germany with her father in 1843, and on May 2, 1847, the two were married in Milwaukee. Shortly thereafter Jacob accepted a job offer in Chicago, where their first child, Lillie, was born in 1848. Late in 1849 the Vollraths returned to Milwaukee, and in 1850 a son, Andrew J., was born. Their third child, Minnie, was born in Chicago in 1852, and in the spring of 1853 the family made their move to Sheboygan.

Sheboygan had just received its charter establishing it as a city, and Jacob Vollrath's name appeared on the first petition submitted to the newly elected officials. The petition, asserting that Joseph Kirkland was charging excessive tolls on his floating bridge across the Sheboygan River, urged the council to buy the bridge and make it a public thoroughfare.

During the 1850s Sheboygan was a booming port city. Its shipyards, cartage lines, hotels, flour mills, and sawmills had all the business they could handle. It was still a frontier town, however. No streets were paved or lighted, little grading had been done on the town plat, and the river had not been bridged except for Kirkland's floating affair. Much of what is the city today was marshy and wet, unsuitable for farming or for building. Because of the lack of waterpower, little manufacturing was done.

The people who settled Sheboygan County were not wealthy. Those who sought to begin factories, such as Vollrath, worked beside the men they could afford to hire. Of the many partnerships Vollrath was to enter before he would go into business for himself, one was with Boehmer and Marling. The three men produced agricultural implements as well as cast-iron cooking utensils.

In 1854 Philipp Meyer, Vollrath's half-brother, arrived in Sheboygan and went to work for the three men for a year or so until the partnership was dissolved. Vollrath then entered into another partnership with W.S. Lathrop and Alfred Newell in the company later known as the Globe Foundry. Meyer was included in the transfer. The Globe Foundry would know many trials before Philipp Meyer became owner and turned the business into a success.

Meanwhile, the Vollraths were adding to their family. A daughter, Mary, was born in 1856, a son, Carl A.W., in 1859, and one more daughter, Nahyda, in 1861. Sheboygan was also growing, at least in population—by 1860 the city counted 4,271 citizens. New stores were opening, and Sheboygan became a stop for traveling salesmen. One of these salesmen, from Chicago, was John Michael Kohler.

Born on November 3, 1844, in the Tyrol Province of Austria, John Michael Kohler came to the United States with his family and settled in St. Paul, Minnesota. From 1865 to 1868 he was employed in Chicago as a clerk, and in 1868 he became a traveling salesman. His job included selling to merchants in Sheboygan, where he met and won the heart of Lillie Vollrath, Jacob's eldest daughter and a teacher in the Union School. The two were married July 5, 1871. John Michael went to work for his father-in-law in the Union Steel and Iron Foundry.

Located at the corner of Ninth Street and St. Clair Avenue, the Union foundry was a successful business, producing plows, railroad frogs, and many small castings used by the furniture factories in Sheboygan. Andrew, Jacob's eldest son, had been working for his father since the age of 12 and was in charge of molding and casting. John Michael was intelligent and quick to learn, quickly becoming an asset to the firm.

Lillie and John Michael began a family almost at once. Their daughter Evangeline was born in 1872; in 1873 a son, Robert J., was added, followed by Walter in 1875, Marie in 1876, Lillie in 1878, and Carl in 1880.

John Michael Kohler, a native of Austria, founded the giant company which bears his name in 1873, the Kohler Company. Today his grandson, Herbert Vollrath Kohler, Jr., is the chairman of the board and chief executive officer of the firm. Courtesy, Kohler Company

LOOKING TO THE FUTURE: THE FAMILY
BUSINESS EXPANDS

The year 1873 was a turning point in the lives of the Kohlers and Vollraths. Jacob, perhaps to stop the growth of nepotism in his company, decided to start a new business producing enameling cast iron and stamped sheet steel. He arranged to sell the foundry to John Michael and his partner Charles Silberzahn.

An announcement of the event was published in the *Sheboygan Times* on December 6, 1873:

Notice is hereby given that the firm of J.J. Vollrath & Co., proprietors of the Union Iron and Steel Foundry, at Sheboygan, Wis., was dissolved by mutual consent on the 26th day of Nov. 1873. All accounts of the said firm will be settled by Messrs. Kohler and Silberzahn, who have succeeded to its business.
J.J. Vollrath
J.M. Kohler

John Michael's business was a success, and by 1879 he was able to buy out his partner. The following April the factory burned. Kohler quickly took on two new partners, Herman Hayssen and John Stehn, and the firm became known as the Sheboygan Agricultural Works. In addition to doing general foundry work, they manufactured straw cutters, feed mills, small threshing machines, and iron fences. By 1881 the firm employed 30 men and transacted business of $30,000 to $40,000 a year.

At the same time, Jacob Vollrath began to make enameled hollowware with six men to assist him. By 1881 he employed 40 men and was grossing sales of $50,000 per year, prompting him to build a new factory. Vollrath was the first manufacturer in the state to use gas extensively for fuel in running machinery.

With a wife and six children to support and business prospering, Kohler began construction of a new home for his family in 1882 on the corner of New York Avenue and Sixth Street, completing it in February 1883. Their happiness was not to continue, however, for less than a month later, on March 2, 1882, Lillie Vollrath Kohler, aged 35, died. Their children ranged in age from two-year-old Carl to 11-year-old Evangeline.

Lillie's sister Mary, her husband John Riess, and their infant daughter Minneline moved into the Kohler home to help raise the children. Minnie, another sister, also helped the family. On November 3, 1887, Minnie Vollrath and John Michael were married at the home of her parents. On October 21, 1891, they had a son, Herbert Vollrath Kohler.

Business was booming. Looking to the future, Kohler decided to move the company from its location at Seventh and Jefferson to a new area. He chose a site about four miles west of Sheboygan in an area called Riverside, which had just been platted by its owner, Nic Balkins. Local businessmen thought the plan outrageous and said it would be too far out in the country to be profitable. His partners must have agreed. In 1901 the name was changed from Kohler, Hayssen & Stehn Manufacturing Company to J.M. Kohler Sons Company. Construction at the new site was begun and the plant began operating in October 1900.

A month after the opening John Michael was dead at the age of 56. The *Sheboygan Daily Journal* of November 6, 1900, said:

In the demise of Mr. Kohler, the city of Sheboygan has sustained an irreparable loss, one that will be felt by every citizen in Sheboygan. He has been identified with the growth and advancement of the city for the past 30 years and has lent his aid and influence to every movement that has for its object the betterment of his home city.

In December 1900 the new plant was totally destroyed by fire. The business returned to its old location while the company was rebuilt.

When Jacob Vollrath "split" his business in 1873, the porcelain enameling of cast iron was being used in the United States to some extent. However, Jacob knew that German industry held the secret to the success of the process. He was too old to return to Germany to learn the process, so Andrew, who was 23 and spoke fluent German, was sent abroad to learn the secret.

While Andrew was in Germany, Jacob, who was still sharing his business quarters with Kohler, decided to move. A new building was erected on a block of land bounded by Fifth and Sixth streets

In 1874 this building housed the Sheboygan Cast Steel Company on Michigan Avenue at Fifth Street. Built for Jacob J. Vollrath, the company's name was changed to the Jacob J. Vollrath Manufacturing Company in 1884, and this building became the first building of the firm. Courtesy, Vollrath Company

Jacob Vollrath sold his first enameled ware from a horsedrawn cart driven house-to-house. The reenactment of the event was for a parade in Sheboygan in the early 1900s. Courtesy, Vollrath Company

and Huron and Michigan avenues. He renamed his business the Sheboygan Cast Steel Co.

Andrew returned in 1874 and father and son tested the secret formula. They repeated the testing time after time without success and finally concluded that some vital part of the process had been overlooked. There was nothing to do but send Andrew back to Germany. When Andrew returned the second time, the process was theirs. The samples they produced were of excellent quality.

By 1886 the company, which had been renamed the Jacob J. Vollrath Manufacturing Co., was expanding and now covered the entire block. It was one of the largest plants in the country devoted to enameled sheet steel ware. Jacob also purchased 30 acres of land along the Lake Michigan shoreline, where he would build a home and park.

His family had expanded. Andrew had married Anna Liebl in 1879, Mary and John Riess were married in 1880, Carl and Laura Imig in 1890, and Nahyda and Rudolph Weimer in 1893.

Unfortunately for the future of his family and business, Jacob brought John Riess and Rudolph Weimer into the company after their marriages. The two men were valuable additions to the company but their presence complicated family relationships.

Jacob Vollrath died on May 15, 1898. His will named his wife Elizabeth as his sole heir to "have, hold and enjoy free from accountability during her natural life." However, the fourth clause in his will stated that:

Upon the demise of my wife, the entire estate shall then be divided into six equal parts ... one part to the children of my deceased daughter Lillie Kohler, in equal shares and the others to my children, Andrew J., Carl A.W., Minnie, wife of John M. Kohler, Mary, wife of John

R. Riess and Nachita D. Vollrath . . . provided, however, that my said sons Andrew J., Carl A.W. and my son-in-law John R. Riess shall have the right to purchase from the other heirs their respective shares of the Jacob J. Vollrath Manufacturing Co. . . . at the actual value thereof . . .

None of these bequests could be dispersed until the death of Elizabeth, but the division of the estate would become a source of trouble for the family in the future. John Michael, by his marriages to both Lillie and Minnie, became the major heir. He would control one-third of the estate, while the rest of the family each received a one-sixth share.

The right to purchase stock from the other heirs was given to John Riess as well as to Andrew and Carl, a privilege not extended to the other two sons-in-law. In effect, John Riess became a "third" son.

Andrew became president after his father's death but, unlike his father, who held all of the authority, Andrew had to answer to the future stockholders. In *The Vollrath Family History*, written in 1980, Jacob Vollrath noted:

Under these conditions the circumstances at the company could only change for the worst. One imagines that in short order Andrew began to give vent to his feelings in no uncertain terms and at will with some well-honed barbs aimed at John Kohler and possibly in the direction of John Riess.

The initial chafing was soon transformed to a turbulent intolerance—the pressures they all worked under became genuinely intense.

The next few years were to be tragic for both families. On August 6, 1904, Carl Kohler mistakenly drank carbolic acid and was dead within the hour. He was 24 years old. Almost a year later, on August 4, 1905, his brother Robert, president of the J.M. Kohler Sons Company and 36 years old, was found dead in his bed by his mother. The tragedies continued. On New Year's Eve, 1905, Carl A.W. Vollrath's eldest daughter, Lillie, died; on October 20, 1906, John Riess, husband of Mary Vollrath, died, followed on November 6, 1906, by Elizabeth Vollrath, aged 84.

With the death of Jacob's widow, the terms of his will would now be met and the break between Andrew and the rest of the family would become a reality. The heirs, exercising their rights under Jacob's will, bought him out.

Walter J. Kohler, son of John Michael Kohler and grandson of Jacob J. Vollrath, was president of the Kohler Company after the death of his father. He also served as governor of the state of Wisconsin from 1929 to 1930. Courtesy, Vollrath Company

At the age of 56, Andrew found himself unemployed for the first time since the age of 12. Using the money he had been paid for his share of the company, Andrew started his own business just north of the city, naming it the Vollrath Company. His brother Carl A.W., now president of the Jacob J. Vollrath Company, took legal action, and Andrew was forced to change the name to the Porcelain Enameling Association of America.

Andrew was now in direct competition with his brother and sisters. Although the company became successful almost immediately, Andrew enjoyed the success only a few years. He died in 1913, leaving the business to four of his sons, Walter, Andrew, John, and Jacob.

Walter Vollrath became president, a position he would hold for 50 years. His son Walter J. Jr., would succeed him after his death in 1964. In 1923 the company's name was changed to Polar Ware, and in 1928 the switch was made from porcelain enameling to stainless steel.

In 1965 a plant in Searcy, Arkansas, was purchased, which at the time was the second-largest manufacturer of stainless steel sinks in the country. In 1986 Polar Stainless Products of Searcy was purchased by the Kohler Company.

Today the Polar Ware Company, headed by Andrew's grandsons, occupies a 50-acre site north of Sheboygan and manufactures stainless steel products for restaurant and hospital industries.

Jacob's second son, Carl Vollrath, became president of the Vollrath Manufacturing Co. after Andrew was forced out. Operations were continued at the same location until about 1910, when a new plant was built at the company's present site on the west side of Sheboygan. The name was changed to the Vollrath Company.

The death of John Riess was a heavy blow to the company. Knowledgeable about all aspects of the business, Riess would have been a great help to the new president. Carl had one person he could count on for help, however—Walter J. Kohler, his nephew, who continued to represent his father's interest in the company.

The Vollrath Company continued to grow in size and scope, its one major competitor being Andrew's firm. Both companies utilized identical techniques and both turned out excellent products. By the 1950s, when the enameled ware business began to phase out, both companies had switched to stainless steel and diversified.

After the death of his father and brothers, Walter Kohler, aged 30, became president of the J.M. Kohler Sons Company. He held the position until becoming chairman of the board in 1937, and was succeeded as president by his brother Herbert V. Kohler.

"A GARDEN AT A FACTORY GATE"

Of all the accomplishments of Walter Kohler, perhaps the most lasting was the planned development of Kohler Village, a small settlement that had grown near the factory at Riverside and was incorporated in 1912. Not wanting the village to become a factory town, ugly and haphazard, Kohler began touring the leading garden city projects in the United States, England, and Europe. The results were incorporated into a village plan of wide streets with provisions for schools, churches, parks, and homes. The platting of lots large enough to permit gardens, trees, and flowers around each home led to the title "A Garden at a Factory Gate."

Much of the land reserved for parks and schools was given to the village by the Kohler family. In addition, many homes were built by the company and sold at cost to employees. A mutual building and loan association was begun to finance workers' homes. The stately American Club was built in 1918 as a residence for single men who worked at the company. It would become home for many immigrant workers who would live there and attend company-sponsored naturalization classes.

In 1920 Walter Kohler built a home in Kohler, calling it Riverbend. His former home in Sheboygan was given by the family to the Prescott-Bayens Post of the American Legion as a clubhouse in memory of Walter's brother Carl, who had served in the Second

The Wisconsin National Guard was called out on July 27, 1934, to protect the Kohler Company and villagers after a mob of several thousand persons attacked company buildings and the recreation hall of the village. Two men were killed and many were wounded in the rioting. Courtesy, Sheboygan Press

Riverbend, the stately home of Governor Walter J. Kohler, was built along the Sheboygan River in the village of Kohler. The English Tudor residence is listed on the National Register of Historic Places and in 1984 was given to the National Trust for Historic Preservation by the children of John M. Kohler and Julilly Kohler, grandchildren of Walter J. Kohler. Courtesy, Sheboygan Press

Wisconsin Volunteer Division in the Spanish American War. In 1928 Walter was elected governor of Wisconsin. He served a single term and returned to Kohler in the midst of the Great Depression.

The distressing economic conditions of the time resulted in a strike against the company in July 1934. Twelve days after the start of the strike, riots broke out, resulting in the death of two men and the wounding of many more. The National Guard was called in to restore peace. When the company resumed operations, an employees' union was established, the Kohler Workers' Association, or KWA. The KWA would last 20 years.

On April 21, 1940, Walter J. Kohler died. He had dedicated 50 years of service to the Kohler Company and to the communities in which he lived. His brother Herbert would guide the company for the next 30 years. Under his tenure the firm would grow from a modest concern to a far-flung business with subsidiaries in Canada and Mexico and a pottery at Spartanburg, South Carolina. Herbert was perhaps overshadowed by the fame of his brother Walter and by his nephew, Walter Jr., son of Walter, who served three terms as Wisconsin governor from 1951 to 1956.

Herbert V. Kohler, son of John Michael and Minnie Vollrath Kohler, took over leadership of the Kohler Company upon the death of his brother, Walter, in 1940. He guided the company through the war years and a bitter strike in 1954. Courtesy, Kohler Company

STRIKE!

It was during Herbert Kohler's presidency of the company that one of the nation's longest and most bitter strikes occurred. The strike began in 1954 and resulted in the United Auto Workers becoming the representative of the Kohler workers. Charges and countercharges flew between company and union representatives. The strike was not confined to the company but boiled over into the county as well. Kohler was the largest employer in the county, so no one could remain neutral. Families were split apart, with sons against fathers and brothers against brothers as the strike dragged on until 1962.

Economic progress of the county practically came to a halt while the strike was in progress. Sheboygan County became a place to avoid, and any building project was complicated over the use or non-use of Kohler plumbing ware. The scars resulting from the bitterness have slowly healed, but the county is poorer for having lost many families who moved away because of the strike.

The strike was to have an unexpected side effect for the Kohler family. Walter Kohler, Jr., was employed at the company while his father was president. Enlisting in the navy the day after Pearl Harbor, he served his country until 1945. He returned to the company briefly and in 1947 became president of the Vollrath Company.

Walter Jr. acquired a taste for politics when he worked in his father's gubernatorial campaign and ran as a delegate to the 1948

This picture shows the picket line that was formed in front of the Kohler Company in April 1954. It was the nation's longest and most bitter strike. It finally came to an end in 1960. Photo by Harold Bogenhagen. Courtesy, Sheboygan Press

Republican National Convention. He polled more votes than any other delegate and was endorsed by the Republican Party as their gubernatorial candidate in 1950. One of Wisconsin's most popular governors, Kohler served three terms.

In 1953, when a strike seemed imminent at the Kohler Company, Walter Jr. divested himself of his Kohler shares. In 1962 he charged that he had been misled as to the worth of his stock, and a court fight ensued. The *Milwaukee Journal* of January 4, 1962, reported:

The quiet hatred which has rent one of Wisconsin's foremost families for more than a decade now suffuses a federal courtroom in Milwaukee . . . Nobody will say how far back the bad feeling goes, but those close to the family say it extends at least as far as World War II.

THE DYNASTY TODAY

Herbert Kohler died July 28, 1968, and passed the leadership of the Kohler Company to his son Herbert V. Kohler, Jr. Walter Kohler, Jr., died on March 21, 1976, passing the presidency of the Vollrath Company to his son Terry Kohler. Under the dynamic leadership of these two men, both the Kohler and Vollrath companies continue to grow and prosper.

Vollrath has diversified over the past several years. In addition to its food service products, the company produces walk-in freezers and coolers and has a Memphis, Tennessee-based health-care division that produces plastics as well as stainless steel items. Another division of Vollrath is North Sails, the largest maker of racing sails

Herbert V. Kohler, Jr., pictured here, is the chairman of the board and chief executive officer of the Kohler Company in Kohler, Wisconsin. Photo by Aida Studio. Courtesy, Kohler Company

in the world. North Sails made the sails for the yacht *Stars and Stripes,* which brought the America's Cup home in 1987.

In 1977 Herbert V. Kohler, Jr., announced a 50-year "Master Plan" for the orderly growth and development of the village. The next 10 years saw much of the plan put into effect. The aging American Club was refurbished and turned into a luxury hotel with magnificent conference halls and dining rooms. A Sports Core was constructed with tennis courts, swimming pool, exercise rooms, and dining facilities near Wood Lake, which had been created for the 50-year plan.

River Wildlife, an unspoiled wilderness area for hunting, hiking, and winter sports, was added. Woodlake Market, a unique grocery store that features specialty shopping areas, opened in 1986. The market anchors a shopping complex that will eventually contain 50 stores. A Peter Dye-designed golf course called Blackwolf Run is scheduled to open in the spring of 1988, and plans are in progress to construct an additional 18-hole course.

The Kohler Company has also forged ahead with new plans. In 1986 Kohler announced the purchase of Baker, Knapp & Tubbs, Inc., a Chicago-based furniture manufacturer and distributor. In November, plans to purchase eight plants, product lines, and operations of Jacob Delafon, a leading plumbing manufacturer headquartered in Paris, France, were announced. Five of the Delafon plants are in France, with one each in Spain, Morocco, and Egypt. In December Sterling Facet Co., a subsidiary of Kohler Company, purchased Polar Stainless Products of Searcy, Arkansas.

Besides running successful companies, the Kohler and Vollrath families have been generous to Sheboygan County and to the state of Wisconsin with their gifts and endowments. Among their many contributions are the beautiful Vollrath Park and Bowl in Sheboygan, site of graduation exercises for Sheboygan's North and South High Schools; John Michael Kohler State Park adjoining Terry Andrae State Park south of Sheboygan, now combined and named Kohler-Andrae; the restored Old Wade House and Butternut House in Greenbush; and the John Michael Kohler Arts Center and the Friendship House, both in Sheboygan.

The Five Diamond-rated American Club at Kohler, Wisconsin, was built in 1918 to house male immigrants who worked at the Kohler Company across the street. There were 110 rooms to accommodate them, along with a cardroom, barbershop and bowling alley. In 1978 the American Club was placed on the National Registry of Historic Places. Remodeled and renovated, the hotel opened in 1981 as one of the state's most luxurious hotels. Courtesy, Sheboygan Press

Chapter V

THE RISE OF COMMUNITIES

The earliest settlers of Sheboygan County considered themselves residents of Sheboygan. There was no distinction as to where they lived, whether it was along the lakeshore, the rivers, the harbor, or in the interior of the county. The only difference between Sheboygan and Sheboygan Falls during the pioneer period was in calling Sheboygan "the Mouth" and Sheboygan Falls "the Falls."

A letter written in 1845 by Dr. Elisha Knowles to his wife, Olive, in Harmony, Maine, explained the early settlers' enthusiasm for the region:

I traveled over Vermont, New York, Michigan, Indiana and Wisconsin, and have at last made up my mind to stop in Sheboygan—it is very healthy soil, good air, solubrious, no disease . . . the society here is good for a new place—all temperance folks, in fact the most so

This bird's-eye view of Sheboygan Falls in 1880 shows the river, streets, and prominent places of business and worship. Photo by Beck & Pauli of Milwaukee, Wisconsin. Courtesy, Sheboygan County Historical Research Center of any place I have seen in my travels.

I have rode a hundred miles since I came on horseback and have seen some choice land, sublime in the extreme. The Sheboygan River is one of the most beautiful rivers I have ever seen—water pure as christal—a quick sliding current—banks not deep but good water power at the falls.

We have in our village about thirty houses, 2 saw mills, one grist mill, one lath machine, one shingle machine, one furnace, two blacksmiths, six joiners, one store very full, one shoeshop, large tavern building will be completed June next! We are six miles from the mouth of the Sheboygan River where there is another village growing upon the lake shore very thriving and will one day be our harbour.

As settlement of the county increased, small villages sprang up, serving the surrounding areas as trading centers. A journey of 10 or 15 miles on the uncertain roads of the territorial period was an all-day affair, one that was not taken lightly and only urgent business would necessitate a journey away from home. Therefore, towns were begun at likely places—at a dam site on a stream or river, by an intersection of two roads, or, later, along the railroad.

CASCADE

Cascade, the oldest village in the county, began on the territorial road built to Madison in 1846. Two men, James Preston and the Reverend Huntington Lyman, searching for a good location to develop a water-powered mill, traveled the road until they came upon the cascades of the Milwaukee River. Here they built a sawmill and laid out a village plat of 40 acres. Houses were constructed and Cascade developed rapidly, with a large number of settlers coming from Canada.

One of Cascade's most noteworthy settlers was Marium Clark, wife of Rufus Clark, a Canadian immigrant. Marium's story is typical except for the fact that she lived to the age of nearly 103. Known throughout the county as "Grandma Clark," she was esteemed for her sweet disposition and serene manner. During the last years of her life her birthday became a celebration for the village.

Marium Worth was born on May 1, 1811, at Stanstead, Canada, a granddaughter of a soldier of the American Revolution. In February 1829 she married Rufus Clark and they continued to live in Canada, where their six sons and six daughters were born. In 1855 the family emigrated to Wisconsin, traveling by boat. Their landing in Sheboygan took place during a terrible storm which shattered every window in the ship and threatened to capsize it. During the voyage a two-year-old daughter died and another daughter died two days after they landed.

Settling on a farm near Cascade, in the town of Mitchell, the Clarks became a typical pioneer family carving a farm out of the wilderness. Two sons, Calvin and Luther, served during the Civil War, returning home safely at its end. Rufus Clark died in 1872 and Marium continued to live on the farm. When she died in 1914, Marium was the head of a family that included six children, 35 grandchildren, 35 great-grandchildren, and one great-great-grandchild.

Because of its central location in western Sheboygan County, Cascade became the natural trading center for the towns of Mitchell, Lyndon, Scott, and Sherman. Located on the stage route out of Sheboygan, it was an important center for travel before the railroad was built. The first industries to be built were Preston's sawmill, a gristmill, and Joseph Bear's general store. A post office was established in July 1849. A persistent story told from generation to generation is that Abraham Lincoln stayed overnight at the Lyndon House in Cascade while on his way to Madison.

In 1866 fire destroyed the business district of the village, a disaster that, when coupled with the railroad bypassing Cascade, was a blow from which the village never really recovered. Businessmen rebuilt, however, and by 1880 Cascade had two hotels, a drugstore, hardware store, three blacksmith shops, one cheese factory, two gristmills, and three churches.

In 1914, 70 years after Cascade was founded, it was incorporated as a village with a population of 338. In September 1915 the Cascade Fire Department was organized. An active community booster, the department helped to sponsor Cascade's centennial in 1948. Thousands of people from the county helped celebrate with two parades, a band concert, fireworks, and the crowning of a centennial queen. Twenty-five years later Cascadians celebrated their 125th anniversary in much the same way.

In 1980 Cascade had a population of 615. Lovely Lake Ellen, just a half mile from the village, is the site of recreational activities. The Kettle Moraine Vineyards, started in the mid-1970s by Don and Lani Parson, is one of only three grape wineries in the state and the first in Sheboygan County.

GREENBUSH AND GLENBEULAH

Greenbush also had its beginnings because of a road. In 1852 the Fond du Lac Plank Road reached the Wade House, established in

1844 by Sylvanus Wade, and a settlement grew around the inn.

Elizabeth and Thomas Cole settled on a farm near Greenbush in 1845. They had emigrated from England, where four of their five sons were born. When Elizabeth died in December 1894 at the age of 89, she was one of the oldest settlers of the county. Four of the five sons had become ministers. The eldest, the Reverend John D. Cole, was serving in Beloit, and his brothers the Reverends Jabez, Jesse, and Thomas also had parishes.

Greenbush was well on its way to becoming a proper town when the Sheboygan and Mississippi Railroad laid tracks to Glenbeulah two miles away. Indignant citizens of Greenbush held a mass meeting to protest but to no avail. The *Evergreen City Times* of July 7, 1866, quoted Fond du Lac's *Commonwealth Reporter*:

The village of Greenbush is stricken with blight, owing to the fact that the travel with teams from Sheboygan to Fond du Lac is almost entirely dispensed with, and to the building up of a rival town in Glenbeulah two miles below, where the railroad at present terminates.

Greenbush, which remains unincorporated, is the site of Old Wade House State Park where the Butternut House and the Jung Carriage Museum are located. Summer brings many visitors who tour the old inn and its surroundings and take a ride in one of the carriages.

The first house built in what was to become Glenbeulah was erected by Donden Ferguson in 1848. In 1850 Hazael Clark began a farm, a part of which became the village of Glenbeulah. Clark and William Pool purchased the waterpower site and built a sawmill.

In 1857 Captain Joseph Swift with his two sons-in-law, James

Glenbeulah, gateway to the Kettle Moraine State Forest, is seen here in 1927 with its unpaved main street and single street light. Today the streets are paved and well lit, while the village retains it charm amidst the beauty of the Kettle Moraine. Courtesy, Sheboygan County Historical Research Center

Dillingham and Edwin Slade, together with Dillingham's father, Stephen, formed the Swift, Dillingham Company to operate a store, a flour mill, and a sawmill.

By the late 1850s the prospects for the village becoming a railroad site were imminent. Edward Appleton, contractor for the railroad, purchased land for a town and platted it in 1859. Appleton named the site Beulah after his mother and prefixed it with Glen for its location in a narrow valley of the kettles. The village was the terminus of the railroad until 1869, and a stage line carried passengers and mail to Fond du Lac. The first blow to the community came when the railroad reached Fond du Lac and the stage lines were no longer needed.

Swift, Dillingham was the most important manufacturer in Glenbeulah. By 1880 they were employing 60 hands and their business amounted to $75,000. The firm manufactured all kinds of woodenware—hubs, felloes, cheese and butter boxes, measures, barrel covers, and broom racks. By 1884, however, the virgin timber surrounding Glenbeulah became depleted, and the firm moved to Sheboygan.

The population of the village was over 500 when Dillingham moved, five times the size in 1860; by the time the village incorporated in 1913 the population had shrunk to 298. Nearly 100 years later, in 1980, it was 423, still shy of the 1884 figure. The village is no longer the important industrial center it had been in the 1870s, but it enjoys the distinction of being the northern gateway to the Kettle Moraine State Forest.

"THE TALE OF TWO VILLAGES"—AMSTERDAM AND CEDAR GROVE

Sheboygan County has several communities whose history might be called the "tale of two villages." Amsterdam and Cedar Grove are two that vied with each other, Amsterdam becoming a ghost town to the benefit of Cedar Grove.

Amsterdam was the summer site of Ohio fishermen who stayed in the towns of Holland and Wilson while fishing Lake Michigan. Gilbert Smith, one of the fishermen, settled along the lake in 1850. In 1852 he platted the village of Amsterdam and built a pier to accommodate sailing vessels. The community grew to include four stores, three saloons, a blacksmith shop, and a barrel factory.

A mile or so inland, in 1847, a small group of Dutch settlers, under the leadership of the Reverend Dominic Pieter Zonne, arrived at what is now Cedar Grove. The Reverend Zonne built a log house and presented it to the settlers for a church. The church served as a magnet for Dutch immigrants, uniting them into a community. The Reverend Zonne named the settlement for the large number of cedar trees in the area.

The roadway of the Milwaukee Lake Shore and Western Railroad was laid in 1872 and a depot built in Cedar Grove. This sealed the fate of Amsterdam. Her citizens moved their village. A cavalcade of 22 ox teams carried the log buildings of Amsterdam up the hill to Cedar Grove.

By 1880 the village had three dry-goods and grocery stores, three shoemaker shops, two harness shops, two hardware stores, a saloon, a cigar factory, and two grain elevators. Cedar Grove was incorporated in 1899.

On February 1, 1929, fire destroyed over 200 feet of business property fronting on Main Street, wiping out the Cooperative Exchange Elevator and several businesses and damaging the Equity building and W.W. Ramaker's soft drink parlor. Firefighters from Cedar Grove, Belgium, Oostburg, Random Lake, Kohler, and Sheboygan Falls fought the blaze, aided by a Chicago and North Western locomotive dispatched from Sheboygan to remove freight cars from sidings adjoining the doomed buildings. The village had no water system and the losing battle had to be fought with chemicals and water carried to the scene by hastily organized bucket brigades. Damages exceeded $75,000 with no salvage value.

A second disastrous fire occurred in 1957 when an oil tank truck collided with a freight train and exploded, causing heavy damage to the feed mill, meat market, and several of the 13 rail cars. Residents for miles around heard the blast, and a pall of dark smoke was visible as far away as Sheboygan. The Cooperative Exchange again suffered the most damage. Over 1,100 firemen from Cedar Grove, the town of Holland, Oostburg, Random Lake, Port Washington, Sheboygan Falls, and the Sheboygan area fought the blaze.

Cedar Grove, whose 1980 population was 1,420, has sponsored a Holland Festival yearly since 1947. Citizens slip into their wooden shoes and colorful costumes and wash the streets. When the streets are clean, the Kloppen Dancers perform and are followed by a parade. The smell of worstebroodjes permeates the air, and visitors may eat Dutch food, visit the Het Museum, buy handiwork at the art fair, and enjoy another ethnic festival of the county.

WINOOSKI AND ONION RIVER

In 1844 the Thaddeus Harmon family settled on a farm in the town of Lyndon. Their only neighbors were a camp of some 200 Indians who lived along the Onion River. Two years later James and Lucinda Stone and their family settled on land one mile west of the Harmons. Other families soon arrived and a settlement was begun on the Onion River which Stone named "Winooski" for another Winooski on an Onion River in Vermont.

Stone became postmaster of the first post office in the town of Lyndon in 1853. Winooski flourished and in 1875 consisted of a

The settlement of Winooski is seen here as it appeared in 1877. Across the mill pond is the old Sheboygan County Insane Asylum with its exercise compound enclosed by a high board fence. Winooski was a busy place with a saw mill, grist mill, blacksmith shop, general store, dance hall, post office, cheese factory, hop house, creamery, cooper shop, potash plant, and a shoe shop. Courtesy, Sheboygan County Historical Research Center

sawmill, gristmill, general store, village hall, cooper, blacksmith and woodworking shops, a cheese factory, and a dozen houses. The population was 88.

Winooski became the home of Jonathan Walker, who tried to revive the abandoned Spring Farm Settlement in the town of Mitchell. In a letter to Charles Hazelton of Littleton, New Hampshire, Walker wrote on March 9, 1855:

I have therefore bought sixty acres of good lands within a quarter of a mile of a small village and am now on it myself, and am disposed to share it with such practical reformatory friends as may be disposed to come here . . .

Spring Farm was never revived and Walker eventually moved to Michigan.

In 1876 Glanville Jewett constructed a building to care for the insane of the county who, until this time, had been housed in the county jail at Sheboygan. On the night of February 19, 1878, the building caught fire and burned. Four of the 17 inmates burned to death, and Jewett died in April as a result of the fire. The structure was rebuilt, and Jewett's wife managed the asylum until a new one was built near Sheboygan in 1882.

Winooski slowly faded away when the railroad was built to Waldo. Today only a historical marker and cemetery preserve its memory.

The settlement of Onion River rivaled Winooski. The first settler was H.L. Hutchison, who, with his family, located there in June 1846. Soon a sawmill was built on the river, and a post office was begun in 1850. By 1880, with a population of 80, the village had a gristmill, store, cheese factory, wagon shop, blacksmith shop, and two hotels. In 1871 the Milwaukee and Northern Railroad was built a half mile west of Onion River. Norman Harmon and Eugene McIntyre bought 80 acres of land on both sides of the track and platted a new town, naming it Lora. Later the railroad company named it Lyndon Station. This name was confusing because of another Lyndon Station in Juneau County, and the name was changed once more to Waldo, in honor of O.H. Waldo, the railroad president.

The rivalry between Onion River and Waldo continued. The residents of Onion River insisted that their mail be brought to their part of the village and distributed from the old post office boxes in Whiffen's store, although the post office had been moved to Waldo in 1878. But the railroad exerted too strong an influence, and Onion River eventually became a part of Waldo. The new village became a shipping center for livestock and grain. In 1889 and again in 1894 there was talk of making Waldo a junction point on a railroad linking the Chicago, Milwaukee, and St. Paul line with Sheboygan. Neither project was realized. Waldo was incorporated in 1923, and today practically no one remembers the village of Onion River.

A prime business near the village is the Waldo Orchards. In 1923 Arno Meyer purchased a four-acre site and planted apple and cherry trees. Almost every farm at this time had a small orchard, and Meyer with his two sons, Frederic and William, sprayed their neighbors' trees while harvesting their own fruit. In 1944 Meyer purchased 40 more acres. A dairy barn was converted into a parking and sales area. With the purchase of an additional 40 acres in 1959, dwarf and semidwarf trees were planted, and today over 30 varieties of apples are grown. Pears, plums, and sweet and tart cherries are also grown on a pick-your-own basis.

The orchards are shown off at blossom time and during the fall harvest by the Frederic Meyer family, who give free tractor-trailer rides. Approximately 3,000 schoolchildren visit the orchard each season, touring the packing room, the cider mill, and the sales room, where they taste the cider and eat apples.

Although Waldo is the smallest village in the county, having a 1980 population of 416, everyone in the county knows its name, thanks to the widespread popularity of the orchard.

HOWARDS GROVE

In the town of Herman, two more villages, Millersville and Howards Grove, eventually joined together and incorporated, becoming Howards Grove.

The township was detached from the town of Sheboygan Falls in 1850 and named Howard for its first postmaster. In 1851 the name was changed to Herman. First settled by Lippers in 1846, the land that would become Millersville was purchased by Henry G. Mueller, who laid out and sold lots for a town named Mueller Villa. This name was later corrupted to Millersville. In 1854 Mueller built the first grist- and sawmill on the Pigeon River, and a cheese box factory was later built in conjunction with the sawmill.

F. Beckfeld, the first person to settle in Howards Grove, built the Washington House in 1849. Herman B. Howard also built a hotel and guest house, later adding the post office to the hotel.

Many of the villagers today are descendants of the pioneer settlers. William Damrow purchased land in Millersville in 1900 and built a tavern on the village corner known as the Millersville House. The tavern, today known as Doro's, is still owned and operated by the fourth generation of Damrow's descendants.

As Millersville expanded northward and Howards Grove south-

ward, the two villages were destined to meet, incorporating in 1967 as Howards Grove-Millersville. The combined village became the fourth largest in the county. In 1971 village residents voted to shorten the cumbersome 24-letter name, the longest in the state, to Howards Grove. The largest and fastest growing village in the county, Howards Grove reached a population of 1,838 in 1980, an 84.2 percent gain since the 1970 census.

Another small settlement in Herman is the unincorporated village of Franklin. In 1880 the village contained two taverns, two stores, two cooper shops, a pottery, cheese factory, and wagon shop. It is best known today as the site of Lakeland College, begun in 1862 as a German college and theological seminary by the Reformed Church.

RAILROAD TOWNS

Before the Milwaukee, Lake Shore and Western Railroad traveled through the northeastern part of the town of Holland in 1873, there was a small settlement called Oostburg, named for a town in the Netherlands. Advised that the railroad would soon be built west of his store, Oostburg businessman Peter Daane realized that his business was in jeopardy. Purchasing land two and one-half miles north of Oostburg, he built a depot and presented it to the railroad. Naturally, the tracks were laid to the depot. Daane built a grain and produce warehouse close to the track and a general store near the crossing. The name "Oostburg" traveled to the location along with Daane.

By 1880 the village had a post office, two general stores, two hotels, two shoemaker shops, a furniture shop, a harness maker, and a cooper shop. Today Oostburg is a prosperous village with a 1980 population of 1,647. The Dutch heritage of its citizens is perpetuated by marriage and community activities centered around its four churches.

Adell also owes its existence to the railroad. In 1873 Christian Gersmehl laid out lots along the railroad and named the place Sherman. It was later named Sherman Station but eventually became Adell. In 1880 it had a post office, two stores, a blacksmith shop, a hotel, and about 15 houses. The 1980 population was 545.

Random Lake, another railroad town, grew out of a settlement along the lake established by John Carroll in 1848. Although the shore of a lake would appear to be an ideal townsite, no village was built until 1870, when the Wisconsin Central Railroad went through the area. The first building erected was the depot. The town was named Greenleaf after E.D. Greenleaf, financial agent of the railway. The name was soon changed, however, to conform with the name of the lake. The town was platted by Guido Pfister in 1872. Growth of Random Lake was constant and rapid. By 1880, with a population of 260, the village had a public school, three hotels, one livery stable, a lumberyard, saloon, wagon shop, and two blacksmiths.

A prominent business operated by three generations of the Orth family from 1869 to the mid-1940s was the natural ice business. The Orths began their business in Milwaukee but as that city grew they became concerned about preserving the purity of their product. When Random Lake became linked by railroad to the major cities to the south in 1878, the business was moved there. It became a major winter industry for the area, employing more than 100 workers from the village and nearby farms. Five ice houses were needed to store the tons of ice that were cut from the lake. Boxcars transported the ice to dealers in Milwaukee, Chicago, and other places. The business was discontinued in 1945.

Random Lake has long attracted fishermen and tourists to the area. The 1980 population was 1,287.

LAKE COUNTRY

Probably the most beautiful lakes in the county are Crystal, Elkhart, and Little Elkhart. Located in the town of Rhine, in the heart of the kettle moraine area, these lakes provided no special attraction to the early settlers, who were interested in farming. Rhine was considered "northern Wisconsin" during the pioneer period, and the lakes were remote and difficult to reach.

It was not until the railroads reached Glenbeulah and later Fond du Lac that the lakes began to enjoy popularity. At first families came by carriage and camped along the wooded shores. In 1872 the Milwaukee and Northern Railroad reached Elkhart Lake, and the area became a mecca for vacationers from cities such as Milwaukee, Chicago, and St. Louis.

Landowners around the lake converted their homes or built cottages to accommodate summer guests, as noted by the *Plymouth Review* of May 22, 1873:

Elkhart Lake is one of the most delightful of the many places of summer resort in Wisconsin which we have seen and it is fast becoming the most popular. The establishment of Elkhart station on the Milwaukee and Northern Railway will be a great convenience to the patrons of the Lake, making the point accessible entirely by rail from Milwaukee without change of cars. The number of people who will visit Elkhart the coming summer will undoubtedly double that of last season, and in view of this many desirable improvements have been made and are now in progress for their accommodation and entertainment.

This picture shows an ice cream parlor at Crystal Lake, an old shopping ground for the interurban streetcar seen here with its passengers. Courtesy, Sheboygan County Historical Research Center

The Lester Laun Furniture store in Elkhart Lake is seen here in the mid 1930s. Laun was president of Laun Lumber and Furniture Company which he owned and operated from 1936 until the late 1960s. This picture shows wicker and bentwood rockers hanging from the walls to accommodate more furniture. Courtesy, Peter Laun

Mr. Marsh, proprietor of the Swiss Cottage, has enlarged, rearranged and refurnished the house in fine style and is making preceptible improvements in the grounds, drives, etc. . . . A steamer, numerous sailing-boats, skiffs, etc. are at the service of visitors, fishing and hunting is afforded on and near the Lake; and a post office just established there affords the great conveniences of quick, daily mails . . .

Besides the Swiss Cottage there are numerous private boarding-houses affording excellent accommodations, among which may be mentioned the delightful residences of E. Tallmadge, H.I. Davidson, Peter Sharpe and Mr. Stewart, some of whom this early in the season have guests who will remain during the summer.

The village of Elkhart Lake was platted by William Schwartz in 1875. By 1880 the village had several stores, a blacksmith shop, and the only grain elevator in the township. The popularity of Elkhart Lake increased as more people began summering there. Hotels were soon built, including Sharpe's, Schwartz's, Pine Point, Siebkins, and Osthoff's.

The most ostentatious buildings were erected in 1890 for Wilhelm Gottfried, a retired millionaire brewer from Chicago. Named Villa Gottfried, his holdings soon encompassed 400 acres. Part of this land was used as a stock farm for horses and cattle. There was also a park for deer and elk, which roamed freely throughout the

Villa Gottfried, a replica of one located on the banks of the Rhine River in Germany, was built in 1890 by Wilhelm Gottfried, a retired Chicago brewer. After his death in 1902 it was purchased by Joseph Wolf, another Chicago millionaire. The villa was demolished in 1949 and the furniture was sold at a public auction and the land sold for lots. Courtesy, Sheboygan County Historical Research Center

area, and a driving track. The grounds also included a greenhouse and palm house for exotic flowers and a theater where performances of German plays were given twice a week. Gottfried kept a steam and sailing yacht in a boathouse on the lake near a floating cottage and pavilion. The estate was broken up and sold after Gottfried's death.

Besides the prime attraction of the Victorian hotels with their spacious grounds and gracious atmosphere, Elkhart Lake also boasts its own racetrack, Road America—an irresistible lure to the greats of auto racing and their fans. Drivers from rank amateur to world champion drive the twisting, climbing four-mile course, which is known as "a bit of European race track" in North America. Road America, which brings millions of dollars into the county annually, is the site for such prestigious events as the IMSA Camel GT races, the CART Indy Racing Series, the American Motorcyclists Association Camel Pro Series, and the Nissan/SCCA Chicago Region June Sprints.

Racing on public roads around Elkhart became popular in the early 1950s, when prominent drivers from all over the country converged on the resort town to race their exotic cars around the lake and through the village. However, a state statute forbidding racing on public roads was enforced, so a hilly 500-acre enclosed track with four macadam miles going nowhere was constructed. The first feature race, held in September 1955, was won by Phil Hill, who became the first American driver to win the World Driving Championship in Grand Prix competition.

THE CHANGING FACE OF SHEBOYGAN FALLS

Sheboygan County has two other cities besides her namesake, Plymouth and Sheboygan Falls. The oldest, Sheboygan Falls, is also the smallest, with a 1980 population of 5,253. Sheboygan Falls, traditionally a center of manufacturing, was outdistanced by her sister city Sheboygan in manufacturing and population, but Sheboygan Falls' base of industry is still strong and supports a bustling community.

The village received its charter on April 1, 1854, and by 1857 boasted eight sawmills. A variety of manufacturing was carried on: wooden suction pumps, clothes reels, chair stuffing and cabinet furniture, fanning mills, carriages, plowshare castings and steam engines, sashes, doors and blinds, and four hub and spoke factories.

German immigrants settled in Sheboygan Falls as well as the surrounding county, and the flavor of the most temperate Yankee village in the country slowly changed, becoming more Germanic in character. The year after temperance leader Charles Cole died in 1867, two breweries were begun.

The 1967 Can-Am Race at Road America in Elkhart Lake, Wisconsin, was witnessed by 53,000 people. Established in 1956, Road America drew thousands of people to Elkhart Lake on a Road America weekend. Courtesy, Sheboygan County Historical Research Center

The first foundry between Milwaukee and Green Bay, started in 1846 by Horace Trowbridge, for many years remained the only one. The waterpower supported the only woolen mills in the county—the Sheboygan Falls Woolen Mill, begun in 1861 by William Prentice, and the Riverside Woolen Mills, built in 1865. The two mills were eventually purchased by G.H. Brickner and combined into the Brickner Woolen Mills, which became the largest employer in the village. The mills were closed after World War II and have remained vacant, awaiting a developer's renovation of the fine brick complex located in the city's downtown historic district.

The oldest industry in the city and county is Richardson Industries. The founder of the company, Joseph Richardson, brought his family, along with his brother-in-law Egbert Burhans, to Sheboygan Falls in 1845. The two men began a sash and chair factory in the

The warp room of the Brickner Woolen Mills was just one of many processes the wool passed through from sheep to finished product. The giant mill occupied one acre of land in downtown Sheboygan Falls and at its peak, furnished employment for hundreds of people. The mill was closed around 1945. Courtesy, Sheboygan County Historical Research Center

village. In 1848 they built a sawmill on the Mullet River, and from this small beginning Richardson Industries evolved. Burhans died in 1853, and the business was carried on by Richardson and his sons.

Joseph and his wife, Caroline, had 13 children. The three eldest, Jairus, William, and Egbert, worked with their father until the Civil War. Jairus was killed at the Battle of Chickamauga, and at the war's end William and Egbert bought into the business, which was renamed J.S. Richardson and Sons. A younger brother, John, also joined the firm. In 1876 Joseph retired from active management of the firm, which then consisted of a chair factory, cheese box factory, planing mill, and lumberyard.

Today the fourth and fifth generations of Richardsons are connected with the firm, which still manufactures chairs along with other fine furniture. The lumberyard, which features one of the largest selections of building materials in the county, has been expanded to include a branch in Sheboygan.

This bird's-eye view of Plymouth in 1879 shows the Mullet River winding around Plymouth as the Sheboygan and Fond du Lac Railroad still bisects the city today. Photo by Beck & Pauli, Milwaukee. Courtesy, Sheboygan County Historical Research Center

In 1983 Joseph Richardson II, president of Richardson Industries, supervised the renovation of an 1894 building in the downtown historic district. Once a grocery store, the refurbished building now houses Richardson's Furniture and Gift Emporium.

Another major manufacturer is the Bemis Manufacturing Company. Organized in 1925 the company took over the vacant buildings of the White Wagon Works. Known worldwide for its manufacture of toilet seats, the company expanded into plastics in 1954. Today, in greatly expanded quarters in the city and in a new plant west of the city, Bemis manufactures wooden household products, particularly for the bathroom and kitchen applications. It also produces health-care products, humidifiers, and kitchen cutlery. The company, the recipient of the Governor's Export Achievement Award, exports its products to Europe, the Middle East, the Caribbean, the Far East, Australia, and New Zealand.

Sheboygan Falls today is a modern, progressive city with a population fast approaching 6,000. The city has five parks, an auditorium that seats 1,800, a fine public school system, and one parochial grade school. A YMCA building, constructed in 1981, hosts a variety of activities. Of the six churches in Sheboygan Falls, the First Baptist, chartered in 1838, is the oldest church in the county.

The diversified manufacturing base of Sheboygan Falls pro-

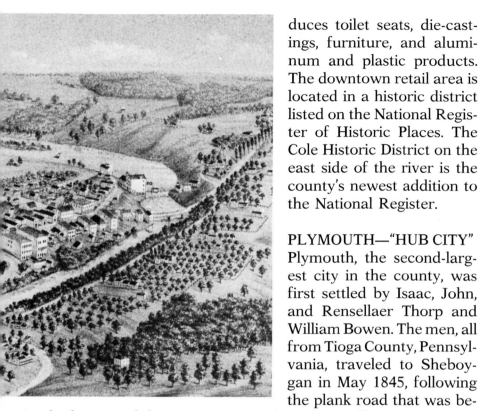

duces toilet seats, die-castings, furniture, and aluminum and plastic products. The downtown retail area is located in a historic district listed on the National Register of Historic Places. The Cole Historic District on the east side of the river is the county's newest addition to the National Register.

PLYMOUTH—"HUB CITY"

Plymouth, the second-largest city in the county, was first settled by Isaac, John, and Rensellaer Thorp and William Bowen. The men, all from Tioga County, Pennsylvania, traveled to Sheboygan in May 1845, following the plank road that was being built to Fond du Lac. Camping along the Mullet River they investigated a cold spring they had been told about. The men decided the area was too stony for farming, so they returned a short distance and built the first log house in the township.

In a few weeks they had cleared enough land to plant corn, potatoes, buckwheat, and garden vegetables. In July they were joined by Henry Davidson and his family. Davidson settled near the springs and built a tavern called the Cold Springs House. The plank road soon became well traveled, although it was known as "the worst road in the world."

Davidson's son Thomas is credited with naming the city "Plymouth" after the city in Connecticut where his first love died.

In 1846 Davidson sold his tavern to John Taylor, who enlarged it. The Cold Springs House, which became one of the best known hostelries on the Fond du Lac Plank Road, was also the center of social gatherings, political conventions, lectures, and other activities.

The village of Plymouth was laid out in 1848 by the county surveyor, H.J. Cowan, who was hired by Taylor and Horatio Smith, owners of the land. In 1851 a brother-in-law of Smith's, Martin Flint, hired surveyor Edmund Bixby to plat another town just east of Plymouth, which he named Quitquioc. The stage thus was set for the "Quitquioc War," which was fought with words between the rival

The Laack city block was built in 1889 by Henry C. Laack. Among the ornate buildings seen on this block is the ageless centerpiece of downtown Plymouth, the hotel, now 52 Stafford Street, which can be seen on the left of the picture. Courtesy, Sheboygan County Historical Research Center

townsite promoters. The two towns were basically one, and the fight revolved around which name it should be called, Plymouth or Quitquioc. In 1851 a petition was presented to the state legislature asking for the name "Quitquioc." The name became law, but at the next session the Plymouth faction demanded a law to restore the original name. The 1852 legislature reversed itself, and the village became Plymouth again.

The feud was also fueled by the politics of the two main combatants, Horatio Smith and John Taylor. The two had been friends and business associates, but they became competitors and bitter rivals. Smith was a Democrat and Taylor a Republican, and the citizens of Plymouth/Quitquioc sided with one or the other.

The Quitquioc House, built in 1850 by Flint, was purchased by Davidson's son, Henry P., in 1851. The hotel had three stories with a dance hall on the upper floor. The music for the Fourth of July dance held there in 1852 was provided by the Cole Band from Sheboygan Falls. Its leader, John Beekman Cole, composed the "Quit Qui Oc March" for the occasion, adding more fuel to the fire.

Residents had their mail addressed according to the name they favored, but the story is told that the postmaster, who was a Plymouth man, would pick out the mail addressed to Plymouth and throw the rest back into the mailbag, saying, "There's no such place as Quitquioc."

Each faction had its own school, and when meetings were held to combine the two, fighting broke out again. Finally, in 1866, the schools were consolidated, and a new school named Union was built. In 1874, when Smith was appointed warden of the Wisconsin State Prison at Waupun, the Quitquioc War ended. Today "Quit Qui Oc" is known only as the name of the high school annual and a golf course at Elkhart Lake.

Of the many people who contributed to the success of Plymouth, the Schwartz family was outstanding. Michael Schwartz emigrated from Germany with his sons Carl, John, and William in the early 1850s. Michael was a miller and a blacksmith and taught his sons the trades. Carl and William established the second industry in Plymouth in 1854, a blacksmith shop. In 1856 they built a foundry on Mill and Stafford streets, and William built the Brickbauer flour mill south of Plymouth. In 1865 he built the Central Roller Mills and a sawmill on the Mullet River, later adding a cider and a planing mill.

John and Carl began a hub and spoke factory in 1867 on the property now occupied by 52 Stafford Street. The brothers turned out wagons, hubs, felloes, and spokes, with the production of hubs their chief product. The factory was so successful that Plymouth was dubbed "Hub City," a nickname it sometimes uses today. Although the factory is long gone, Plymouth, in the center of the county, remains a hub.

William wasn't through building. In 1872 he graded the roadway for the Milwaukee and Northern Railroad from Plymouth to Kiel, stopping in Elkhart, where he owned a large farm, to build the depot. Then he constructed the Hotel Belleview (now Siebkens) and the Lake View House, which was doubled in size by brother John and is now the Schwartz Hotel. Back in Plymouth in 1878, William built a factory south of the present utility that saw the beginnings of five furniture factories—Schwartz and Preussler, A.W. Schram Chair, Phoenix Table, Plymouth Chair, and Crescent Chair.

While all this building was going on, the brothers did not neglect their civic duties. Carl served as assessor for two terms, and William was elected town treasurer in 1860 and 1862, serving three terms

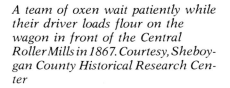

A team of oxen wait patiently while their driver loads flour on the wagon in front of the Central Roller Mills in 1867. Courtesy, Sheboygan County Historical Research Center

as county supervisor from 1879 to 1888.

Plymouth never incorporated as a village but instead went right to city status. The state legislature passed a special act of incorporation and granted the city a charter in 1877. The first mayor was Otto Puhlman, who served from 1877 to 1886.

One of Plymouth's most colorful characters was William "Dynamite Bill" Gardner. Born in Door County in 1887, Gardner became a "powder monkey" in a stone quarry at the age of 12. After moving to Plymouth, he blasted stone for farmers around Elkhart Lake. He served two years as an army private in World War I with the Rainbow Division's demolition squad, returning to Plymouth and more dynamiting. His skills became widely known, and when a blasting problem arose, Gardner was sent for. His toughest job was blasting a channel through a generator station along the Fox River at Kaukauna, successfully coping with water pressure and leaving the nearby bulkhead dam and pumps undamaged.

Only once was Gardner injured. In 1933, while he was blasting concrete at Miller's Guest House near Plymouth, onlookers pressed too close, distracting his attention. The resulting premature blast sent him to Wood Veteran's Hospital for 10 months.

Gardner's biggest blast was not of his making. In 1946 he had parked a trailer load of dynamite in a field southeast of the Plymouth Hospital. A young boy, out target shooting, took aim at a bird perched atop the trailer. The resulting blast was heard for miles around the county, shaking houses and businesses and shattering windows in a wide area. Plymouth businesses on Mill Street lost over 90 plate-glass windows.

Dynamite Bill remained active until the late 1950s. In 1956, when he was over 70, he took down twin 56-foot silos at the Bemis Manufacturing Company at Sheboygan Falls.

Plymouth in 1980 had a population of 6,027 and has been steadily growing. Major industries include General Telephone Company's eastern divisional headquarters, as well as numerous companies connected with the cheese industry. Valley View Medical Center, with its adjacent extended-care facility, is run in conjunction with Sheboygan's Memorial Medical Center. The city was the first in Wisconsin to build low-rent housing for senior citizens. Eight churches offer worship facilities, while excellent school systems include a public and two parochial grade schools.

Chapter VI

THROUGH TWO WORLD WARS

A new wave of immigration beginning in the 1890s and continuing until World War I brought new families to Sheboygan County. These immigrants included the Volga Germans, the Slovenians, Croatians, Lithuanians, Greeks, and another migration from the Netherlands. Nearly all of these people, including the Dutch, settled in the city of Sheboygan.

The Volga Germans were descendants of Germans who had settled near the Volga River in Russia during the reign of Catherine II. Never assimilated into the Russian culture, they began leaving Russia in 1866 when the government canceled their military service exemption. The first of the Volga Germans arrived in Sheboygan in 1892, but their greatest period of immigration was from 1908 to 1912. Sheboygan's Volga Germans remained in the city and quickly

The grading of New Jersey Avenue at South Fifteenth and South River streets in Sheboygan was done by horses pulling drags. The three-month project was completed on August 1, 1893. In the background is the main building of the Schreier Malting Company. Courtesy, Sheboygan Press

Music, dancing, and food highlight the annual Greek Fest sponsored by St. Spyridon Greek Orthodox Church each year at Sheboygan's Kiwanis Park. Thousands of gyros, shish kebabs, Lucanikos, salads, and deep-fried honey puffs are consumed by an appreciative public. Courtesy, Sheboygan County Chamber of Commerce

Facing page top: This picture from an unknown artist shows a log cabin built by William Paine and Col. Oliver Crocker in 1834. The two men also built a sawmill at the site of the first rapids of the Sheboygan River but failed to secure legal title to the property and lost it to William Farnsworth the following year.

Facing page bottom: Sheboygan had visions of becoming famous as a mineral bath and health resort after a well dug in Fountain Park in 1875 was found to contain healthful minerals. The Sheboygan Mineral Water Company was given the exclusive rights to bottle and sell the water, and enjoyed a national reputation and market for many years. This plate was an advertising gimmick given to customers in the early 1900s. Courtesy, Alice Timm Collection

became citizens of the United States. On June 21, 1942, 7,000 Volga Germans celebrated the 50th anniversary of their arrival in Sheboygan with ceremonies at Vollrath Bowl.

The first Slovenians came to the county in 1891 and continued immigrating until 1914. The Croatians followed in 1901. Although the language of the two groups is distinctly different, both groups helped organize Saints Cyril and Methodius Church in 1910 and support its parochial school which was begun in 1916. Each year a Slovenian Day is held to keep alive their culture and customs.

During the latter part of 1898 Lithuanians began to arrive, a great many of them young, single men who married after they settled in Sheboygan. By 1903 the group was large enough to establish and support the Immaculate Conception Church.

The Greeks who arrived in the late 1800s were from Arcadia and Messinia, provinces of southern Greece. Unskilled workers from a predominantly agricultural society, they found employment in the furniture factories and tanneries and on the railroads. Settling in an area south of Indiana Avenue between Seventh and Fourteenth streets, their settlement was dubbed "Greek Town."

The Greeks organized an Orthodox Community in 1902, serviced by a traveling priest from Chicago. In 1904 members began raising funds to purchase land and build a church. St. Spyridon was completed in 1906 and became an important center for Greeks in this part of the country. Today the church serves some 200 members in Sheboygan as well as Greek families in Green Bay and Manitowoc. Every year a Greek festival is held at Kiwanis Park with the 50-odd families of St. Spyridon's hosting as many as 20,000 people. Greek food, music, and dancing make the festival one of the most successful events of the summer.

A popular explanation for the name "Sheboygan" is credited to an Indian chief who once lived here. It seems that the chief had many sons but longed for a daughter. Overjoyed when his wife became pregnant again, he was certain the child would ge a girl. Upon returning from a hunt, he was met by his wife with a baby in her arms. Her words to her husband were reported to have been "She a boy again!

Left: The Judge Taylor house, located in Taylor Park, is one of two parks operated by the county. The house is now the Sheboygan County Museum that stores and displays the artifacts of the county. Courtesy, Sheboygan County Historical Research Center

Below: This cheesemaking mural painted by Charles Winstanley Thwaites, a Milwaukee artist, adorns the post office in the city of Plymouth, Wisconsin. The mural was installed in 1941 when Plymouth was known as "The Cheese Capital of the World." Thwaites shows the many stages of the cheesemaking process, starting at the source--a cow seen through the open window of the cheese factory. New Deal art, as it is sometimes called, decorates post offices and public buildings throughout the United States, one of the happier legacies of the Great Depression. Photo by Dawn Jax Belleau

Old Main, the oldest building still standing at Lakeland College is the cornerstone of the Mission House Historic District listed on the National Register of Historic Places. Photo by Marilyn Payne

"De Visch" or "The Fish" windmill is located at Windmill Park in Cedar Grove. "De Visch" was built to help perpetuate the rich heritage of the village. The windmill is a replica of a South Holland grain mill. Its overall height is 28 feet with a height to the top of the sail of 46 feet. It was built in 1968 and was presented to the village by the Cedar Grove Booster Club. Photo by Sheboygan County Chamber of Commerce

Above: Colorful sailboats congregate at Sheboygan harbor. Courtesy, Sheboygan Area Chamber of Commerce

Left: This harbor scene shows boats landing along the shores of Lake Michigan. Courtesy, Sheboygan County Chamber of Commerce

Right: The boardwalk of the Rotary Riverview Park, along the river in Sheboygan, is a popular place to view the harbor, watch the boats sail, or just to take a nice leisurely walk. Courtesy, Sheboygan County Chamber of Commerce

Below: Spring-fed Lake Ellen at Cascade is the site of summer and winter activities in the town of Lyndon. Photo by Marilyn Payne

This fishing pier and lighthouse overlooks the vastness of Lake Michigan. Photo by Paul H. Henning/ Third Coast Stock Source, 1987

Bright yellow tulips in front of the American Club in Kohler, Wisconsin, highlight the corporate headquarters of the Kohler Company. Courtesy, Kohler Company

Above: This aerial picture shows the sprawling Kohler Company and the American Club in the left hand corner of the picture. Courtesy, Kohler Company

Right: The John Michael Kohler Arts Center hosts exhibits, art classes, and other special events throughout the year. Photo by Paul H. Henning/Third Coast Stock Source, 1987

Seen here is Sheboygan's City Hall/Police Station. Photo by Paul H. Henning/Third Coast Stock Source, 1987

Pictured here is the First Evangelical Lutheran Church in downtown Sheboygan. Photo by Paul H. Henning /Third Coast Stock Source, 1987

Built in 1910, the S.S. Cyril and Methodius Catholic Church is one of the oldest churches in Sheboygan. Photo by Paul H. Henning/Third Coast Stock Source, 1987

GREENBUSH KETTLE

THIS AREA WAS IN THE INTERLOBATE VALLEY BETWEEN THE MORAINES OF THE GREEN BAY AND LAKE MICHIGAN GLACIERS. MANY MASSES OF STAGNANT ICE WERE COVERED BY OUTWASH GRAVELS. WHEN THE ICE MELTED, KETTLES WERE FORMED. THIS VERY DEEP DEPRESSION WAS LEFT BY THE MELTING OF SUCH A LARGE ICE MASS.

Greenbush, located in the northern part of the Kettle Moraine State Forest, is the site of recreational activities throughout the year. The Kettle Moraine is of glacial origin and is characterized by a rough broken terrain of wooded hills, swamps, marshes, glacial lakes, and gravelly uplands. Photo by Marilyn Payne

IMMIGRATION TRIGGERS EXPANSION

The city grew and expanded to accommodate the influx of new families. In 1895, 4,230 men and women were employed in 37 major factories, the two plants of the Crocker Chair Company being the largest. The "A" plant employed 375 while the "B" plant had 400. Mattoon Furniture was second with 600 employees. Other major manufacturers were Phoenix Chair, Sheboygan Chair, American Chair, Spratt Chair, and Dillingham.

Among the many civic improvements were the new bridges on Eighth and Fourteenth streets. After much hassling and debate a sewage system was installed, streets were paved and electrified, electric streetcars began operating on city streets, a public library was begun, and additional schools were erected. In 1890, 2,400 children registered for school. Two years later the figure was 7,387. In 1893 the city's population of 23,000 supported 102 taverns.

On April 23, 1898, President William McKinley issued a call for 125,000 volunteers to assist the regular army in a war against Spain. On April 28 Company C's Second Regiment of the Wisconsin National Guard, including 155 Sheboygan County men, traveled to Camp Harvey near Milwaukee, where they were mustered into the service of the U.S. army. The county volunteers were under the command of Colonel Charles A. Born, mayor of Sheboygan.

The Spanish American War was an almost bloodless affair, but conditions in the army camps in Puerto Rico generated much sick-

Crowds gathered beside the railroad tracks for the return of the Spanish American War veterans in September 1898.

ness, which was the cause of death for many soldiers. Willie Trier, a Sheboygan member of the regimental band, died in a hospital in Ponce, and Albert Doege died shortly after his return to Sheboygan. Doege-Trier Camp No. 66 of the Spanish American War Veterans was named in honor of the two men.

The soldiers returned home on September 9, 1898, and the city council appropriated $250 for a reception. The *Sheboygan Daily Journal* of that day headlined the event:

Every society in the city, every man, woman and child will join in giving honor to the brave boys in blue—the best company of the best regiment of soldiers on the face of the earth. Everybody should decorate, the big unearthly screech of the Mattoon whistle will give signal three hours before the expected arrival of the saviours of this grand, glorious country.

SHEBOYGAN GREETS THE NEW CENTURY

A new century was beginning. Horse racing was the rage and several city streets were blocked off so that horses could be trained. The telephone had come to the city in 1881 but was still a novelty. Electric lights first flickered in 1888, but homes were lighted by gas or candles and kerosene lamps. The city boasted a library, a hospital, and five schools. For entertainment there was the Opera House, the Concordia Singing Society, Turnfests, Saengerfests, Saengerbunds, and bicycling. The interurban was built to Sheboygan Falls in 1900; two years later it extended to Plymouth, and in 1909 it reached Elkhart Lake. In 1912 a new city hall was built.

One of the most disastrous fires to strike the city occurred on December 16, 1900. The Zschetsche Tannery burned at a loss of $120,000, the largest and costliest fire Sheboygan had experienced.

After a typhoid epidemic struck the city in 1908, the city's water supply was found to be polluted. The council had been trying to purchase the waterworks for many years, but the issue remained unresolved. After the epidemic there was no trouble in passing a bond issue, and the city finally had a municipal water system. In 1912 sewer and water mains were laid.

In August 1909 the city held a big party, called a "Homecoming." Anyone who had ever lived in Sheboygan was invited back to see how Sheboygan had grown and matured. Hundreds accepted the invitation, coming from all over the United States to sign the register and comment on the changes time and hard work had wrought. The party was a success, and $1,451.36 was raised for the purchase of library books.

A typical, turn-of-the-century saloon was Weinert's Tavern in Sheboygan. It featured an embossed tin ceiling, a row of spittoons, and the inevitable cigar counter.

In 1914 war raised its ugly head in Europe, and on April 2, 1917, Sheboygan citizens voted on the issue of America entering the war. The result was 17 for and 4,112 opposed. Four days later war was declared, and on September 22, 1917, the first contingent of county men left for training. The *Sheboygan Press* printed the following report of their departure:

Promptly at 8 o'clock this morning the selected men were lined up at Eagles Hall and given their final instructions. A few minutes later, headed by the Maas Band of twenty pieces, and with members of the local exemption board, County Council of Defense, city officials, Spanish War veterans and the new State Guard Company as escorts they marched down Eighth Street to Pennsylvania Avenue.

They marched west to the North Western station where their cars were awaiting them. After saying goodbye to their families and friends, they entrained to Battle Creek.

Of the 2,047 men from the county who served in the army, navy, and marines, 53 died. The returning soldiers came home to Prohibition and the loss of their jobs. The Common Council established an employment bureau to aid the returning veterans.

The next 10 years saw a consolidation of the gains made by the city and county. In 1920 the last of the horses and equipment of the fire department was sold as the department became completely motorized. The park system, enhanced by the gifts of Vollrath Bowl and Park and De Land Park in 1915 and the purchase of Cole's woods (Evergreen Park) in 1918, received land along the river from the local Kiwanis Club in 1924. The new park was named Kiwanis Park.

The county was also busy. In 1924 the County Normal School for the training of teachers was built in Sheboygan Falls. During 1925 and 1926 Rocky Knoll Sanitorium, located in the town of Plymouth, was constructed. Washington School was enlarged in 1925, and plans were made to build a junior high school in 1929.

THE DEPRESSION HITS SHEBOYGAN

The stock market crash of 1929 and the resulting Depression wreaked havoc on the county's economy, as it did worldwide. Many prominent businesses were not able to weather the blow; others managed to hang on—barely. The Westport Steamship Line, which went out of business in January 1930, was the city's last commercial freight carrier by water.

The building of the new court-house in 1933 provided jobs for many residents during the Depression.

Though the private economy was staggering, Sheboygan had several major building projects in the works—the South Side Junior High School in 1930 and Memorial Hospital and the Taylor Park Reservoir in 1931. These projects went ahead as scheduled, providing work for many. In 1933 and 1934 a new courthouse was built.

In the midst of the gloom of the Depression, Charles E. Broughton, editor of the *Sheboygan Press*, wrote an editorial pointing out that the 100th anniversary of the first settlement in the county would occur in 1934. Acting on his suggestion for a celebration, the Sheboygan Men's Association decided to sponsor a "birthday party." For eight days in late August and early September city and county residents put aside their cares and worries to attend Sheboygan's Centennial and Homecoming. The festivities included the dedication of the new courthouse, church services, baseball games, band concerts, speeches, songs by the Concordia and Liederkranz Singing societies, a Labor Day parade and picnic, dances, a reunion banquet, and the burning of city hall bonds in front of city hall.

The years between 1934 and 1940 saw the county's economy bolstered by WPA projects. The federally sponsored construction included North High School, a sewage disposal plant, a new post office, and the Municipal Auditorium and Armory.

As the Depression drew to a close and the threat of war once again loomed, the character of the county changed. Wisconsin's lumber supply had diminished and the furniture industry had grown less profitable. As furniture factories closed, a variety of other industries came to the forefront. They included tannery goods, toys, shoes,

Charles E. Broughton, editor of the Sheboygan Press *from 1908 to 1951, raised the small newspaper to national prominence during his tenure. His series of editorials in the 1930s on cruelty in Wisconsin's mental health hospitals won honorable mention for the Pulitzer Prize. Broughton died in 1956 at the age of 83, but the scores of organizations which had his support and leadership are still going strong today. Photo by Glaeser Studios. Courtesy, Sheboygan Press*

clothing, bread wrapping machinery, enamel ware, malt, and, of course, the cheese industry.

By 1940 practically every street in the city was paved, and a network of concrete or blacktopped highways made every community in the county accessible by automobile or bus. The streetcar and interurban tracks were taken up, and a bus system became the popular mode of transportation.

TOYS INTO TANKS—SHEBOYGAN COUNTY GOES TO WAR

After the Japanese attack on Pearl Harbor, industries in the county, like their counterparts nationwide, turned their skills to the manufacture of materials for war. From the manufacture of sleds, wagons, and tricycles for children, the Garton Toy Company converted its plant to the production of bomb fins and torpedo parts. In 1945 they were awarded the coveted army-navy "E" award for excellence in the production of war materiel, an honor accorded to only 4 percent of the nation's industries. Upon receiving the Army Ordinance banner in 1943 the toy company's chairman of the board, Clarence Garton, spoke for all the residents of Sheboygan:

Surely nobody in their right senses would forget that it has been a great change from making toys to the making of bomb fins, torpedo parts and other war material, but if we are ever to make toys again for free children in a free world, we will have to forego the making of toys long enough to destroy the evil forces that would make our world a prison and rob our children, not only of their toys but of their liberties.

Tillie Strojinc, of the tool and die making department at the Kohler Co., uses a depth micrometer in grinding gauge. Women at Kohler operated lathes, drill presses, and grinders, and became inspectors, checkers, and clerks in the factory during World War II, taking over many of the jobs usually performed by men who were then serving in the Armed Forces. Photo by Kohler Co. Courtesy, Mrs. Ray Schetter

Garton Toy was not the only Sheboygan firm to receive the "E" award. It was also awarded to American Hydraulics for its production of artillery shells, bomb fuses, and airplane and rocket parts, and to the Kohler Company for its precision controls on aircraft, high explosive and

The Vollrath Company began working for the war effort in late 1941 and by August 1942 the company devoted 100 percent of its time to the defense work. A prominent part of their war work was the making of stainless steel canteens. These women manufactured over 12 million canteens during World War II. Courtesy, Vollrath Company

Sheboygan County held many War Bond Rallies during World War II. This Vollrath Company truck, featuring their products, was a part of such rallies. Courtesy, Vollrath Company

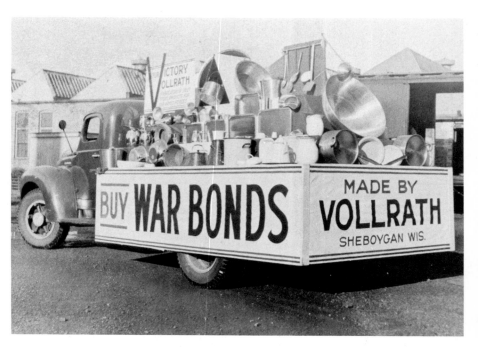

rocket shells, forgings for shells, fuses and piston rings for aircraft, artillery tubes, shell bands, and engine bearings. Two other local firms to receive this award were the Electric Sprayit Company, which made turret assemblies for tanks and generators, fractional motors, and hydraulic devices for aircraft, and the Vollrath Company, for its production of canteens and mess equipment.

A number of other firms in the county also contributed to the war effort. The milk powdering plant at Verifine Dairy converted to drying whole liquid eggs on government contract; 25 percent of Schreier Malting Company's output was turned to making alcohol for the manufacture of synthetic rubber, smokeless gunpowder, pharmaceuticals, and plastics; 75 percent of the Sellinger Glove Company's output went into making rugged gloves for the army and air corps. Optenburg Iron Works made deck sections for LCT landing craft, idler wheels for army tanks, rings for aerial torpedoes and deck houses, and web frames for maritime ships; Paper Box and Specialty made boxes for batteries and shipping of war materials; and the Jung Shoe Company made army shoes. The list was endless —Sheboygan County had truly gone to war.

In 1944 a German prisoner-of-war camp was established on the county fairgrounds at Plymouth. More than 3,000 prisoners were interred in Wisconsin to work at the pea canneries and the corn packing plants. Those quartered at Plymouth were closely supervised under the provisions of the Geneva conference. A barbed-wire fence encircled the encampment, and the prisoners were closely guarded at all times. At summer's end they were moved out.

Slovenian dancers entertain at one of St. Cyril and Methodius Parish's annual ethnic family-oriented Slovenian Festivals. In addition, Sloga, Liberty Lodge 18 of Sheboygan, sponsors an annual Slovenian Heritage Day each fall. Courtesy, Sheboygan County Chamber of Commerce

Some 7,000 Sheboygan men and women served their country in the armed forces, 155 giving their lives. Veterans returning home at the war's end were given a big party complete with parade, speeches at Vollrath Bowl, free beer, and a dance. Retail stores, taverns, clubs, and other places of amusement closed for the day at 12:30 and blowing whistles and ringing bells began the tribute day at noon.

Later that year the city purchased a section of land for a veterans' housing project to ease the housing shortage. The 60 apartments, constructed from barracks procured from the federal government, were occupied as fast as they were built.

The nation's veterans barely had time to settle back into civilian life when the Korean conflict arose in 1950. Twelve servicemen from Sheboygan County gave their lives on that battlefield. Fifteen years later, in March 1965, the county recorded its first casualty of the Vietnam War. Twenty-four more county servicemen would lose their lives in that conflict.

SHEBOYGAN TURNS 100

August 1953 saw the celebration of Sheboygan's 100th anniversary as a city. For one week the city celebrated its birthday with a pageant of history, music, fireworks, and a bratwurst day, which was so successful that it became a yearly affair sponsored by the Jaycees.

Germans brought the recipe for making the succulent sausage to Sheboygan, and it has become the favorite food for picnics and cookouts. In summer clouds of smoke can be seen rising from backyard grills and hovering over parks and picnic areas. The aroma and taste cannot be described but must be savored and enjoyed. One reason Sheboygan County has so many picnics, festivals, and parties is surely a double brat in a hard roll!

One of the most outstanding men in Sheboygan County during the first half of this century was Charles E. Broughton. Few men have left such a lasting mark on their community. Born in Fond du Lac County on October 22, 1873, Broughton became a printer's devil at the age of 11. A newspaper man for the rest of his life, Broughton was called to the editorship of the *Sheboygan Press* in 1907. Sheboygan's population numbered 26,398, and there were already two English-language newspapers being published. The *Sheboygan Press* had a 1908 circulation of 60 and was the least-read paper in the city. It was not an auspicious beginning.

Broughton, however, was a fearless editor dedicated to the protection of people's rights. His readers might not always have agreed with him, but they always knew where he stood on the issues. By 1917 circulation reached 5,000, and the *Press* took over the assets of the *Daily Journal.* In 1921 the *Telegram* succumbed, and the *Sheboygan Press* stood alone in the newspaper field in Sheboygan. In 1951, when Broughton resigned as editor and publisher, the circulation was 25,826.

For nearly half a century as newspaper publisher and radio station owner, Broughton worked for his community and country both privately and publicly. Whether writing editorials to collect funds for the needy or chairing drives such as the disaster relief committee of the American Red Cross, Broughton worked tirelessly. One of his favorite contributions was the founding of the Kiddies Camp for underprivileged children in 1926. The camp, built in Evergreen Park, today is known as Camp Evergreen. He was also instrumental in founding the Wisconsin Elk's Association Crippled Children's Commission.

An outstanding conservationist, Broughton was one of a group of men responsible for the reflooding of the Sheboygan Marsh, a 12,000-acre haven for wildlife. The Sheboygan County Board of Supervisors honored him by naming the wildlife area Broughton Sheboygan County Marsh Park. While serving on the advisory council of the Wisconsin Conservation Commission, he founded awards based on conservation work for the Boy Scouts and 4-H clubs.

In 1946 Broughton was elected Grand Exalted Ruler of the Benevolent and Protective Order of Elks. He was also one of the first seven individuals in the world to receive the Salvation Army Distinguished Service Award. Perhaps the most fitting and meaningful honor was from the city's Common Council, which named the most beautiful and scenic drive in the community—Broughton Drive —for him. Broughton died on October 31, 1956, leaving a legacy of service and commitment to Sheboygan County.

The first Saturday in August is set aside to salute the succulent sausage that made Sheboygan the bratwurst capital of the world. Courtesy, Sheboygan County Chamber of Commerce

Chapter VII

SHEBOYGAN COUNTY TODAY

Sheboygan County grew and prospered because of Lake Michigan. Today, Sheboygan is once again looking to the lake and harbor area for economic development. Lake Michigan remains the open door to the county. The ships carrying cargo and immigrants are long gone, but the area is filled with craft of another kind—charter, sail, fishing, and pleasure boats—which still wait for the Eighth Street bridge to open and close as they sail underneath.

Children enjoyed the water feature at Plaza 8 from the day it was opened. However, the pools were later closed to wading for fear of injury of the children leaping from the platforms and scampering around the different levels. Courtesy, Sheboygan Press

The riverfront and harbor areas of the city are booming, thanks largely to the sport fishing industry. Sheboygan is the home port of more than 60 charter boats, and the business they generate has resulted in an awakening awareness of the lake as a potential resource. For too long citizens have regarded it only as an endless supply of water and a cool place to visit, not as a stimulant to economic

This picture shows the heart of Sheboygan in 1974 before Plaza 8 was constructed and changed the traffic pattern of the city. The Reiss Coal docks and piles of coal are visible in the upper portion of this picture, along the river. The dark, tall building below the coal piles is First Wisconsin Bank. The seven-story building will be retained as a second office tower when City Center is built in 1988. Courtesy, Sheboygan Press

growth. In recent years, however, there has been a resurgence in communities up and down the Wisconsin coast of Lake Michigan as millions of dollars are spent on marinas, hotels, and lakefront development. Sheboygan's 28-room Harbor Inn, built in 1986, has become so successful that owner-developer Darrel Mand is planning a 24-unit addition featuring a swimming pool and exercise area. Plans for a restaurant are also in progress.

Historically, Sheboygan's harbor area has been home to the shanties of the commercial fishermen. While the Great Lakes Fishing Company remains in one shanty, the rest have been taken over by other businesses. A replica of the early shanties has been built to house Dockside, a combination tavern, sandwich shop, and gift shop.

The attraction for new business in Sheboygan is enhanced by Rotary Riverview Park, dedicated in 1983 as part of the city's Riverfront Revival Project. Located along the north bank of the Sheboygan River as it flows into the lake, the park consists of shelters or

The construction of Plaza 8 forced the closing of the main street in downtown Sheboygan and swing streets were thus built around the area. Eighth Street is seen in the center and in the lower left hand portion of the picture fish shanties can be seen along the river. The twin spires near the top of the picture marks Holy Name Church, the first Catholic Church in the city. Courtesy, Sheboygan Press

This picture shows the dramatic water feature of Plaza 8, next to Mead Public Library. The three fingers of water at the top of the feature were added after construction to add interest to the cascading water and to silence critics who disliked the original structure. Courtesy, Sheboygan Press

overviews of the river with terraced walkways leading to the water's edge. Extending along the riverfront is a lighted boardwalk with slips for docking, a favorite with Sheboygan citizens.

PLANNING AND DEVELOPMENT

Until the late 1950s Sheboygan's central area remained the heart of the economic and social life of the county, attracting large banks and savings and loans, theaters, stores, hotels, and restaurants. The buildings, almost without exception, were constructed before or around the turn of the century, and merchants and owners, who faced virtually no competition, found little incentive to keep their places of business up to date.

In 1959 Montgomery Ward closed its five-story department store on Eighth Street, which seemed to presage the serious deterioration of the downtown area. Soon other old buildings were abandoned and torn down to enable their owners to avoid paying taxes on vacant property. A local banker, Robert McCord, founded a "Parade of Progress" under the auspices of the Sheboygan Association of Commerce, a strictly private enterprise that encouraged some sporadic progress. No unified renewal effort resulted, however, and upon the untimely death of McCord the project faded away.

In 1969 a shopping mall was constructed at the western limits of the city, enticing J.C. Penney and Sears to relocate from the downtown area. The completion of Interstate Highway I-43 through the county from Milwaukee to Green Bay attracted shoppers to the shopping malls in these two cities, both only an hour's drive away. Fond du Lac, less than one hour to the west, also drew Sheboygan residents to its malls, draining more dollars from the county.

With the last urban renewal grant ever given by the Department of Housing and Urban Development, the city consulted five different professional renewal firms on the plight of the downtown area. All recommended building an enclosed mall. Lawrence Halprin and Associates of San Francisco, California, was chosen to plan the downtown renovation. Historically, the idea had been to fill every space along the main street with stores. Halprin maintained that this approach was neither economically feasible nor interesting. His idea for the area was a pedestrian-oriented retail, social, and cultural center. This plan relied heavily on open spaces—courtyards, walkways, and park-like gathering places. It also resulted in the razing of 11 more buildings and the destruction of the area's historic traffic pattern.

After 10 years of planning, the state's only downtown pedestrian mall, called Plaza 8, opened in 1976 to mixed reactions. It contained 36 retail outlets, three theaters, seven government buildings, the Mead Public Library, four restaurants and bars, five banks and savings and loans, and numerous professional offices, and a central water feature which provoked controversy. Over 600,000 bricks were laid for walkways, walls, and decorative features. New lighting

Mead Public Library, Sheboygan's award-winning facility, is located in the heart of Plaza 8. A popular place for county residents, Mead is one of the 50 best libraries in the United States. Courtesy, Sheboygan Press

Winter comes to Plaza 8 as trees, shrubs, light posts, and the H.C. Prange store are festooned with lights and ribbons for the approaching holiday season. Courtesy, Sheboygan Press

enhanced the area, and hundreds of flowering trees, shrubs, and bushes were planted. In spite of Sheboygan's frequently cold weather, the mall was not enclosed because of the enormous cost of covering the area.

Though a beautiful setting for a centralized business district was complete, the exodus of businesses continued, leaving the area shy of the necessary stores to satisfy customer demands. The 10 years of planning Plaza 8 had pitted businessmen against landlords and city officials against planners, creating dissension and resistance to the project.

Problems arose the first winter. Shoppers grumbled because their four-lane street was gone and they had to drive around for parking. Accustomed to parking in front of a business, they disliked entering a shop from the rear. Merchants neglected to upgrade the backs of their buildings, and the proposed parking ramp, although funded, was never built. Cold weather caused the bricks on the plaza walkway to heave, break up, and fall apart, a further deterrent to shoppers.

In 1979 Orrin Ericson, a developer from Bloomington, Minnesota, was prepared to invest $13 million to cover the plaza and build the parking ramp. Ericson's proposal hinged on establishing a tax incremental financing district, or TIF. The state legislature was expected to act on a proposal that would expand the allowable uses of industrial revenue bonding by municipalities. However, the legislature adjourned in April 1980 without acting upon the proposal, and Ericson, having some financial problems in Minnesota, withdrew from the project. Another developer, Donald Bergman of Watson Centers in St. Louis Park, Minnesota, tried to arrange building and financing, but formally withdrew his proposals in 1982, accusing the city and merchants of imposing impossible delays.

No new developers could be found to rescue the county from its downward economic trend. Developers cited the high cost of financing, the county's lack of growth, and the concentration of retail activity on the west side of the city as hindrances to further development. They also pointed out the disadvantage of being next to Lake Michigan, which reduced the territory from which to draw customers.

A near deathblow to downtown development came on May 4, 1983, when a freak accident occurred at the H.C. Prange Company. A water main burst, eroding the support pillars of the giant retail firm causing the floors and roof to sag. The Prange Company has been a mainstay of the community since 1887, when Henry C. Prange, his sister Eliza, and J.H. Bitter opened a 30-by-110-foot store on Eighth Street. The store eventually grew to encompass a one-block area and became the second-tallest building in Sheboygan. Shopping "by Prange's" became a county tradition; one could purchase every conceivable item from a packet of needles to a wedding dress, along with a complete array of home furnishings.

Losing Prange's was akin to carving the heart out of Plaza 8. The whole community cheered when H.C. Prange, grandson of the founder, announced that Prange's would rebuild, and in April 1984 a new 97,000-square-foot single-story building was opened to the public.

In 1986 John Livesey of Madison suggested a $60-million development that would include three 100,000-square-foot office towers, a 100- to 200-room hotel and convention center, a department store, and 60 condominiums. He proposed the demolition of downtown buildings along Plaza 8 from Ontario Avenue south to Center Avenue, leaving only Mead Public Library, Trinity Lutheran Church, and the new Prange store standing. The area comprised 35 acres of downtown property covering an eight-square-block area.

The proposal garnered favorable comments and support from the population and city officials. Because of financing problems, the three office towers were combined into two in early 1987 and later scaled down to one, leaving the seven-story First Wisconsin Bank as the second tower. The multimillion-dollar project, called the City Centre, is scheduled to begin in 1988. Livesey is also developing the area north of the shanties in conjunction with the downtown project by building a multimillion-dollar office-retail complex. Construction of five structures began in September 1987.

EDUCATION AND HEALTH CARE

There are eight public school districts in the county, all having independent school systems. In addition, Plymouth has both a Lutheran and Catholic elementary school, while Sheboygan Falls has a Catholic school. More than half of the county's high school graduates go on to some form of higher education. The Sheboygan Area Board of Education, which oversees the city of Sheboygan's school system, was named "School Board of the Year" by the National School Boards Association for its continuing responsiveness to community needs; excellence in relationships between staff, community groups, and individuals; commitment to quality education; and efforts in long-range planning.

There are 12 elementary, three middle, and two high schools in the Sheboygan district. Each one has a guidance counselor, speech and reading therapist, and special programs for the handicapped and learning-disabled. Sheboygan, which pioneered the concept of career education, has a comprehensive vocational program for high school students. The city also supports a Lutheran and Christian high school and several parochial elementary schools.

In 1987 South High School was named one of the top schools in the country, one of only 271 secondary schools in the nation to receive this honor. Awarded a letter of congratulations from Department of Education Secretary William Bennet, the school also received a "Flag of Excellence" and a plaque. Its principal, Gerald Freitag, was also honored as Wisconsin's "Principal of the Year" by the National Association of Secondary School Principals.

The Rehabilitation Center offers rehabilitation services and vocational training to the handicapped of the area. The center also provides a variety of services to business and industry through a sheltered workshop and study programs.

High school graduates may choose from three institutions of higher learning in the county—the University of Wisconsin-Sheboygan Center, Lakeland College, and Lakeshore Technical College. Lakeland established a Lifelong Learning program in 1978 to meet the continuing educational needs of adults in the area, offering classes on campus and in Sheboygan. Known as Lakeshore Technical Institute until 1987, Lakeshore Technical College, a popular vocational school, serves Manitowoc and Sheboygan counties from its Cleveland, Wisconsin, campus. Stephen Portch, inaugurated as the first chancellor of the Sheboygan Center of the University of Wisconsin in 1987, promised in his inauguration speech to provide "the premiere freshman-sophomore education experience in the nation."

Quality health care is provided to county residents by three hospitals, two in Sheboygan and one in Plymouth. The oldest hospital, St. Nicholas, founded by the Hospital Sisters of the Third Order of St. Francis in 1890, is a comprehensive medical-care facility providing all patient services from cardiology to surgery. In addition, it conducts community classes, offers outreach services, and sponsors community events and support groups. A $17-million hospital was constructed in 1979 on Sheboygan's west side.

Memorial Medical Center, founded in 1932, operates a 24-hour emergency center that serves as a poison control center and the base for Orange Cross Ambulance Service. Completely modernized in 1980, the hospital operates a variety of outpatient services and a psychiatric-care unit.

In 1986 Sheboygan Memorial Medical Center and the Valley View Medical Center, established in Plymouth in 1916, formed a joint management corporation to avoid duplication of services. While one individual serves as president of the boards of both hospitals, separate control of operations is maintained by each hospital. Valley View has 24-hour emergency service and offers quality medical care, as does its companion facility.

The Sheboygan Medical Clinic, begun in 1922, moved into a state-of-the-art, 85,000-square-foot building in 1986 on the west side of Sheboygan. The professional staff of more than 40 physicians offers a wide variety of medical services and specialties. The Sheboygan Regional Oncology Center, a $1-million cancer clinic, was also built on Sheboygan's west side in 1987. The 3,000-square-foot clinic is affiliated with Sheboygan Memorial Medical Center, the Sheboygan Clinic, Valley View Medical Center at Plymouth, and Milwaukee's St. Mary's Hospital. The center is one of two cancer treatment facilities in the county—St. Nicholas Community Cancer Care began treating patients in early 1987.

The county maintains three health-care institutions: Rocky Knoll Health Care Facility near Plymouth; Sheboygan County Comprehensive Health Center near Waldo; and Sunny Ridge in the city of Sheboygan. Rocky Knoll was begun in 1926 as a sanatorium for the treatment of tuberculosis. Dubbed the "Haven of Health," Rocky Knoll led the fight in Wisconsin against the once-dreaded respiratory disease, which gradually lost its stigma as physicians made advances in treatment. Surgery and drugs were prescribed instead of complete rest, and patients' recuperative stays shortened from years to months and then to weeks.

As medical advances lengthened people's life spans, the county recognized the need to provide care for the elderly. Rocky Knoll began to shift its emphasis from tuberculosis treatment to geriatric care, adding a new wing in 1972 to house administration offices, a

*Rocky Knoll Health Care facility
was opened in 1926 as a sanatorium to treat tuberculosis. Today,
while still maintaining a section
for TB patients, Rocky Knoll is a facility for geriatric patients. Courtesy,*
Sheboygan Press

cafeteria, and 104 hospital beds. Sunny Ridge, the county-operated nursing facility for the elderly, was constructed in 1960. The 200-bed building was quickly filled, and in 1971 a six-story, 200-bed addition was constructed.

The county also provides care for the mentally and emotionally disabled. The Comprehensive Health Center, opened in 1940 as an acute center and hospital for psychiatric patients, is a nursing home for the chronic mentally ill, the developmentally disabled, and the substance abuser.

PARKS AND LIBRARIES

Sheboygan County supports two parks—Broughton Sheboygan County Marsh and Taylor parks. Taylor is the headquarters for the Sheboygan County Historical Society, which runs the Taylor House on the property as a county museum and landmark.

Named one of the 50 best libraries in the United States, Mead Public Library, founded in 1897, is the center or main library for the Eastern Shores Library System. This cooperative network, consisting of 13 public libraries in Ozaukee and Sheboygan counties, allows patrons to use any public library in the two counties. It also provides a bookmobile service and borrowing privileges to residents of Manitowoc, Calumet, and Fond du Lac counties.

SHEBOYGAN COUNTY—A LINKING OF PAST, PRESENT, AND FUTURE

Sheboygan County has had a rich and varied past. It has witnessed the timbered wilderness tamed and its rivers bridged and dammed. The timber wolf no longer howls, the bear and wild cats have disappeared. A fledgling dairy industry has matured and helped Wisconsin earn its reputation as the "Dairy State" and "America's Dairyland."

Today Sheboygan County is home to over 100,000 people, 70 percent of whom reside in the three cities and 10 villages. The remainder live on farms or in unincorporated villages. Most citizens worship, work, and play within a short distance of their homes; the traffic, congestion, and smog of large cities are unknown. With four distinct seasons, every conceivable recreation is available, from swimming and boating to camping, hiking, cross-country and downhill skiing, snowmobiling, fishing, golf, and tennis.

As residents look forward to celebrating the county's sesquicentennial in 1988, the future looks full of challenge and promise.

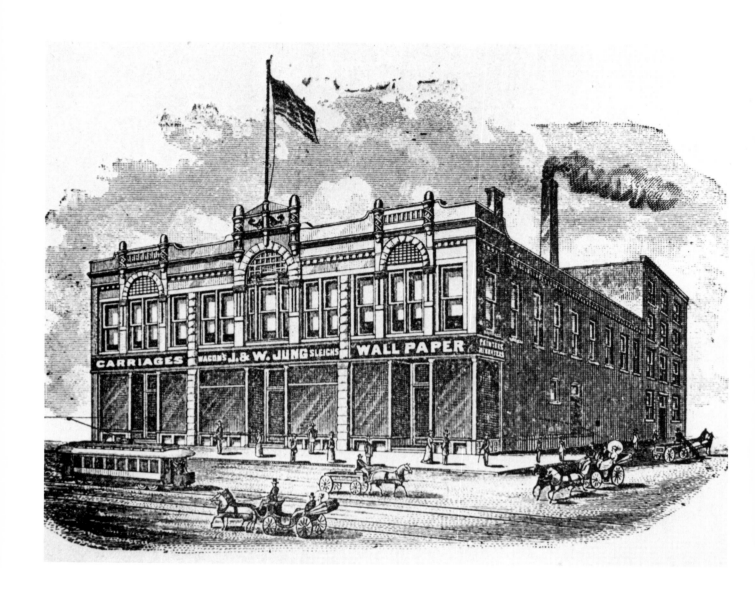

Chapter VIII

PARTNERS IN PROGRESS

In the early 1800s the territory now known as Sheboygan County was an unbroken wilderness inhabited solely by Indians. The first signs of civilization and industry came to the area in 1834, when Colonel Oliver C. Crocker and William Paine built the first sawmill and constructed log cabins. As hundreds of immigrants passed across the city's docks and settled in the lush Lake Michigan countryside, Sheboygan eventually began molding itself into a progressive business community.

On the following pages are the histories and present-day accounts of businesses and industries that have helped to shape Sheboygan into what it is today—a highly diversified commercial county with 1,250 companies providing employment for thousands of men and women.

Many of these businesses keep low profiles. Therefore, their inclusion in this section of the book will be an added premium for those who did not know what these companies were about, and how they came into existence. In fact, until some years ago, Sheboygan County itself was considered a well-kept secret. But due to the variety of its many fine businesses and organizations, the community is becoming famous for its numerous accomplishments—many of which are evidenced by the histories of these companies.

Through the years Sheboygan has also acquired its share of nicknames, such as the Four Cs—Cheese, Chairs, Children, and Churches—Chair City, Land of Contentment, Tree City, the Lake Place to Be, and so on. These monikers have served their purpose; but none adequately captures the heart of what Sheboygan is really about—a place where people are the best resource. For they will carry on the tradition of what their forefathers brought with them from the old country—love for the land and the people who worked together to build a prideful heritage.

Sheboygan County can be proud of what its 150 years have wrought, even though it struggled with adversity and hardship, because it emerged as an economically strong community ready to extend its hand to all who come to settle there.

The organizations whose histories are detailed on the following pages have chosen to support this important literary and civic project. They illustrate the variety of ways in which individuals and their businesses have contributed to the county's growth and development, and are working cooperatively as Partners in Progress to build a better tomorrow, a future legacy for Sheboyban County.

Founded in 1855 by Jacob Jung, J. & W. Jung was one of Sheboygan's largest manufacturers of wagons, carriages, and sleighs.

SHEBOYGAN COUNTY CHAMBER OF COMMERCE

In 1885 five local businessmen organized the Sheboygan Businessmen's Association. More than a quarter-century later the organization renamed itself the Sheboygan Association of Commerce and incorporated. Its first official act under president Ernest W. Schultz was to form an industrial corporation to promote and attract new industry to Sheboygan.

As the city began to flourish, so did the membership of the Sheboygan Association of Commerce. Due to a need for more office space, the organization moved from the German Bank building (after 36 years) into the top two floors of the Security First National Bank building. With plush offices and an attractive porchside restaurant, the association had ample room to conduct business and to hold social functions.

One such social function involved a "mock wedding" ceremony to illustrate the close cooperation between the Sheboygan Association of Commerce and the Lions Club. Miss Association of Commerce (Walter Grasse) was given in marriage by Old Man Association of Commerce (Edwin Koellmer) to Mr. Lion (George Klein). Herbert Jung was best

Sheboygan Association of Commerce club/lounge room atop the Security First National Bank building in 1929.

The Sheboygan County Chamber of Commerce's building and offices (inset) today at 631 New York Avenue.

man, Jacob Jung was maid of honor, Ernest Wolf was ring bearer, and attorney Gust Buchen was minister.

Through the years the association not only changed its name to the Sheboygan County Chamber of Commerce, but also made changes in improving its promotion of Sheboygan County's qualifications as a great place to live, work, and play. Equally important was the chamber's role in legalizing the Elkhart Lake Road Races (now named Road America) and organizing a fishing group that later became known as the Sheboygan Area Great Lakes Fishermen.

The chamber continues to take an effective leadership role in shaping, supporting, and sponsoring the county's future growth. Says Scott C. Wilson, the organization's current president, "Even though today's Sheboygan County Chamber of Commerce is rooted by its history, its vines branch into many present-day accomplishments."

In 1986 the chamber provided direction in community development by working with the Sheboygan Development Corporation to assist 16 local companies in expansion. Other activities include operating a Convention & Visitors' Bureau that brings millions of dollars in tourism and conventions to the area; helping to develop support for downtown renewal, which has led to bringing the Livesey Co. (a Madison developer) to Sheboygan to plan construction of a $100-million downtown enclosed mall; and supporting the Sheboygan County Water Quality Task Force in working with government agencies to better Sheboygan's harbor and river.

The Sheboygan County Chamber of Commerce's future plan of action is not only to expand the area's tourism and convention trade and provide programs that will involve county businesses in the legislative process, but also to continue to build Sheboygan County's tax base and employment base, and to advance the growth of the economy.

ECLIPSE MANUFACTURING COMPANY

Company officers include (left to right) Robert W. Leicht, vice-president/manufacturing; Robert C. Senkbeil, vice-president/marketing and sales; Richard F. Leicht, president; Richard F. Leicht, Jr., secretary/treasurer; and Jeffrey K. Leicht, vice-president/engineering.

In 1939 Fred Leicht, along with his son Kenneth and longtime associate Herbert C. Senkbeil, founded a business that became known as Eclipse Manufacturing Company. They were joined in this venture several years later by Harold Bloedel. The company was formed for the purpose of manufacturing metalworking tools and dies, as well as stamped metal components and assemblies for established local and areawide metalworking industries.

Operations began in a 2,000-square-foot basement in a local Ford automobile dealership at Virginia Avenue and Eighth Street. The small venture experienced continued growth during the ensuing years to the extent that it soon outgrew its available quarters. Ground was broken in the fall of 1948 for construction of a new plant at the corner of 19th Street and Oakland Avenue on Sheboygan's south side. Continued growth has seen various additions to the original plant, and today the operation encompasses in excess of 95,000 square feet of manufacturing, engineering, and office

space.

In 1968 co-founder Herbert C. Senkbeil succeeded Fred Leicht as president of Eclipse Manufacturing Company and served in that capacity until 1974, at which time leadership of the firm went to Richard F. Leicht, a grandson of the founder. Assisting him in running the corporation are fellow officers Robert W. Leicht, also a grandson of the founder; Robert C. Senkbeil, son of the co-founder; and Richard F. Leicht, Jr., and Jeffrey K. Leicht, sons of Richard as well as great-grandsons of the co-founder.

Eclipse Manufacturing Company currently employs 110 people in its full-service, contract stamping operation. Recognizing that its continued success would depend upon maximum development of people skills along with the incorporation of the latest

available technology in its manufacturing operations, the firm has made training and acquisition of that technology two of its prime corporate goals. As a result, Eclipse continues to be recognized as a leader among its peers.

In the late 1970s the firm acquired Kress-Hertel Company, a long-established Sheboygan retail men's clothier that continues to operate under the direction of its president, Howard K. Leicht.

In 1979 Eclipse Manufacturing Company acquired another long-established Sheboygan firm, Optenberg Iron Works, which was founded in 1893 and whose divisions, with an average employment of 90 people, are engaged in fabrication and mechanical contracting. Its Fabrication Division produces heavy steel and alloy fabrications, metal shapes, tanks, pressure vessels, and special projects for the power, petroleum, chemical, metalworking, and construction industries. Its Mechanical Contracting Division, specializing in piping installation and steam fitting, serves the needs of area-wide manufacturing and construction industries.

Several mid-size metalworking presses among 45 similar type production machines to be found in this manufacturing facility.

AMERICAN ORTHODONTICS CORPORATION

The company's business is supplying consumable materials (commonly known as "braces") to the more than 11,000 orthodontists and dental surgeons in the United States and abroad.

American Orthodontics Corporation of Sheboygan commenced operation in 1968 and did $400 of business the first month. It is now

Inside the plant at American Orthodontics Corporation, which ranks in the top five worldwide in orthodontics production and sales.

generally regarded as one of the good places to work in Sheboygan County with just under 200 full-time employees. The firm's offices and research facilities are still located in the original 3,000-square-foot building (formerly the Sheboygan Bandage Corporation) that has since been modernized and expanded to its current size of 16,000 square feet.

An employee turnover rate of practically zero is a tribute to the outstanding employee relations—a review of the payroll records

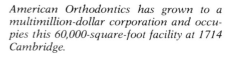

American Orthodontics has grown to a multimillion-dollar corporation and occupies this 60,000-square-foot facility at 1714 Cambridge.

show that several of the very earliest employees are still with the organization. Employees are treated as honest, intelligent persons, and are kept fully informed of anything that affects their job and the company's future. In fact, all employees actually participate in many decisions affecting the direction of the firm. Meetings are held throughout the year on company time with employees to discuss just about anything that needs to be discussed and to keep everyone informed about the organization. It has been amply demonstrated at American Orthodontics that if employees are given the opportunity, the tools, and the encouragement that they do want to work and to perform their job in an above-average manner with pride.

There are no time clocks, and employees are permitted to work a flextime schedule that they can modify without prior notice on a daily basis—provided they put in a minimum of 40 hours each week.

John Viglietti, vice-president, believes people identify with honesty when they are dealt with honestly. He says it develops an atmo- sphere of trust and mutual respect "which means good morale, which equals high productivity, which, in turn, means profitability."

The company produces more than 10,000 individual parts that are assembled in about 100,000 or so different combinations to fit the ever-changing needs of the professional practitioners throughout the world. These products are made from alloys of exotic metals (titanium, palladium) and the more mundane (gold, silver, stainless), as well as ceramic and a great variety of plastics.

Manufacturing techniques include precision milling (to .0003 inch), cutting, forming, stamping, induction and laser welding, soldering, microcasting, and metal injection molding—all to rigid quality standards.

On board are many imaginative and ingenious people with years of experience in working on the cutting edge of technology who are given encouragement to "try something different." At American, this has paid handsome rewards in new products and in market penetration. An example is that 25 percent of the 1986 volume came from new products introduced within the past two years and more than 50 percent from products developed within the past five years.

As a result of ingenious marketing and innovative product developments, American Orthodontics Corporation received the "E" Award in 1977. Three years later the company became the third area manufacturer to win the U.S. Department of Commerce's "E"-Star Award for outstanding ac-

complishments in the field of international trade. This award is given to firms that have shown a large and consistent increase in export sales as measured by the percentage of total sales and the actual sales dollars over a consecutive three-year period. In addition to selling in all 50 states, the company now exports its products to more than 40 foreign countries.

Focus and dilution of effort are important words to the firm's management. It is very important to all who work at American Orthodontics to have and to keep a deep moral commitment to the customer, to the employee, to those who manage the business, and to those who have entrusted their funds to operate the business. The company's president, Daniel Merkel, says, "and you can put those commitments in any order you choose—they are all equally important." He continues, "No matter how large we get, we do not intend to change the basic formula of keeping our operation in balance." By that he means balance between sales, finance, and production, because another key to prosperity is to exercise restraint on the temptation to expand the company too quickly—which

causes many small businesses to fail—and to do things a little bit better, a little bit faster, and for less money than the giant companies in the field. It is obvious that these basic concepts work.

Through the years American Orthodontics Corporation has more than held its own against such giant competitors as Johnson & Johnson, American Hospital Supply, and Bristol-Meyers, and it is currently among the top five in orthodontic production and sales

The first location of American Orthodontics Corporation.

worldwide.

Due to customer demands, the company was forced to expand its physical plant in 1972, 1975, 1980, and 1985. It now owns a modern 60,000-square-foot plant located on the site of the old Legion Park baseball and football stadium.

Due to American Orthodontics Corporation's management, customer, shareholder, and employee balance, as well as being a good corporate citizen—all of which has contributed to the company's success and growth—the firm earned national recognition by being selected as Wisconsin's 1984 Small Business of the Year.

HERITAGE MUTUAL INSURANCE COMPANY

John R. Holden, chief executive officer.

Failure of the Interstate Insurance Company of Madison, Wisconsin, and the need for liability insurance to cover the ever-increasing number of horseless carriages prompted the formation of the precursor of the Heritage Mutual Insurance Company in 1925.

Spearheaded by G.W. Damrow, a Sheboygan insurance agent, 44 incorporators founded the Mutual Automobile Insurance Company of the Town of Herman at Scheib's Hall in the unincorporated Sheboygan County village of Franklin on June 20, 1925. True community spirit was shown by 17 of the incorporators, who pledged what was then substantial financial support to a venture in which they could receive little or no financial return.

Calvin G. Greibe, a Franklin storekeeper, managed the company for its first five years (1925-1930). He was followed by Walter F. Pfeiffer, a Franklin veterinarian (1931-1950); Marvin C. Hessler (1951-1960); and John R. Holden, a Sheboygan attorney (1961-present).

Since 1960 the company's assets have increased from $3.3 million to $170 million, its premium writings from $3.2 million to $120 million, and its surplus from $554,968 to $43 million.

The firm wrote only private passenger automobile insurance in Sheboygan and adjoining counties until 1944, when it received authority to write statewide. At that time its premium writings were $175,318. In 1957 it became the Heritage Mutual Insurance Company. Five years later the firm began writing fire, home owners, and inland marine insurance. Heritage entered the commercial insurance line in 1969; today this accounts for more than half of its writings.

Early in 1987 Heritage announced the formation of Greatway Insurance Company, a wholly owned subsidiary through which it will sell nonstandard private passenger auto and residential dwelling coverage.

Until 1981 Heritage limited its writings to Wisconsin. That year the company began writing business in Iowa and Ohio. In 1982 operations began in Indiana. Beginning in 1987, commercial lines only are being written in the additional states of Minnesota, Nebraska, and Kentucky, initially as a service to Heritage agents in adjoining states. The firm expects to be operational in Illinois in both personal and commercial lines by early 1988.

Heritage has had six Sheboygan County home office locations during its 62-year history: Henry Greibe store, Franklin (1925-1930); Arthur Mauk home, Ada (1930); Dr. Walter Pfeiffer home, Franklin (1931-1947); former Martin Gesch store, Franklin (1947-1960); 2300 Kohler Memorial Drive, Sheboygan (1960-1984); and the newly constructed facility at 2800 South Taylor Drive, Sheboygan (1984-present).

The current home office was designed by Bruce Graham, renowned architect of the international architectural firm of Skidmore, Owings and Merrill, headquartered in Chicago, Illinois. The setting for the 150,000-square-foot building is a landscaped, garden/lake 90-acre area on the southwest edge of Sheboygan, highly visible from South Taylor Drive and Interstate 43.

In addition, Heritage has a full-service office in downtown Cincinnati, Ohio. It also has branch claims offices in Milwaukee, Madison, Green Bay, Wausau, Eau Claire, and Sheboygan, Wisconsin;

The home office of Heritage Insurance from 1947 to 1960.

Heritage Insurance was headquartered in this building from 1960 to 1984.

Today the corporate headquarters (left and below) is at 2800 South Taylor Drive, Sheboygan.

and exempt and nonexempt. Two-thirds of the employees are presently located in Sheboygan. The work ethic of employees in this community is considered by the company as its greatest asset.

Heritage has three noninsurance company subsidiaries, all based in Sheboygan. The Heritage Computer Corporation sells property and casualty insurance software to other insurance companies across the country. The All Lines Insurance Agency is a general managing agency, selling excess/surplus and hard-to-place insurance lines through Wisconsin agents. The Heritage Financial Corporation buys and sells real estate, assists agents in the purchase and sale of agencies, and owns and manages insurance agencies it holds as wholly owned subsidiaries.

Selling low-cost property and casualty insurance with unmatched service to deserving insureds continues to be the objective of Heritage Mutual Insurance Company, as it has been for the past 62 years.

Des Moines, Iowa; and Cleveland, Ohio. At present 910 agencies and 3,934 licensed agents, operating as independent agents under the American Agency System, represent Heritage in the states in which it operates.

The more than 600 Heritage and Heritage subsidiary employees are the real key to the success, growth, and profitability of the firm. Their technical skills, productivity, and dedication are legendary throughout the industry. The work force is about equally divided between male and female,

J.L. FRENCH CORPORATION

J.L. French Corporation produces aluminum die castings and complete engineered assemblies for the automotive industry, and is located in Sheboygan's Industrial Park.

When the company was founded in 1968 by its owner and president, James L. French, it began with a 9,600-square-foot building and 30 employees. Currently J.L. French Corporation has more than 400 employees and more than 200,000 square feet of manufacturing space.

James L. French credits his company's success and industry recognition to a competent, dedicated work force willing to produce quality products at a competitive price with foreign competition.

RIGHT: James and Mary Lou French at the opening of their second addition.

BELOW: Sheboygan's Industrial Park is home to the J.L. French Corporation.

THE POLAR WARE COMPANY

The Polar Ware Company was founded in 1907 by Andrew J. Vollrath as the Porcelain Enameling Association of America.

When the firm was founded it employed approximately 55 people in a 100,000-square-foot factory, and manufactured domestic porcelain-enameled cooking utensils. In this period enameling was considered an uncertainty, and the success of the product depended on the ingenuity and skills of the founder and the capabilities of the work force assembled. Through persistency and dedication, Vollrath became known in the trade circles as "America's pioneer enameler."

Then, in 1913, Andrew Vollrath died, leaving the management of the still-struggling company to his sons, Walter, Jacob, Andrew, Carl, and John. Walter, as president, with Jacob and Andrew as vice-presidents, retained managerial positions and guided the company to success.

With the firm's white enamel-

By the 1930s, when this photo was taken, the firm's name had been changed to The Polar Ware Company and emphasis was beginning to shift to stainless steel utensils.

Andrew J. Vollrath founded the Porcelain Enameling Association of America, predecessor to The Polar Ware Company, in 1907.

ware products being sold throughout the United States and the entire world, the company adopted the slogan "White as the Polar Snow." In 1919, to reflect the quality of its product and the slogan's success, the name of the organization was formally changed to The Polar Ware Company.

While supplying the expanding market for enameled utensils in the hospital and restaurant field, The Polar Ware Company began experimenting in 1926 with a new type of material that would allow development of an innovative new concept of utensil manufacturing. After sufficient progress in its experimentations with a new product, the firm introduced to the world its initial line of commercial utensils manufactured from stainless steel.

Besides the expense, a tremendous amount of missionary work was necessary to successfully market stainless steel materials.

For many years stainless steel was considered a novelty item, something that would soon be a thing of the past.

During and after World War II the general demand for stainless steel products increased to where the production facilities at The Polar Ware Company were strained beyond normal capacities. In 1951, after a long and careful study analysis, the firm made the decision to halt all production of enameled utensils and concentrate completely on stainless steel products.

From 1954 to 1986 Polar Ware was led by Walter Vollrath, Jr., first as president and then as chairman, and Richard J. Vollrath as executive vice-president and later president.

Today The Polar Ware Company, under Christopher Vollrath as president and Walter J. Vollrath III as executive vice-president, manufactures stainless steel food service and medical utensils, and contracted items that are produced to customer specifications in a 180,000-square-foot facility with 140 employees.

SARGENTO INCORPORATED

In 1949 Leonard Gentine, Sr., opened a mail-order gift house and retail cheese store in a small carriage house in Plymouth, Wisconsin, called the Plymouth Cheese Counter. His concept was simply this: to offer smaller-size, convenient, individually wrapped cheese products of Wisconsin and the world.

In 1953 Joseph Sartori joined Gentine to combine their experience, finances, and names to become the Sargento Cheese Company. Sales of the Sargento products went to the A&P Tea Company National Warehouse in Green Bay, from where A&P would distribute the cheese to its 4,200 stores. Other major corporations such as Swift, Borden, Armour, and Wilson also distributed Sargento cheese.

Two years later, in order to expand capacity, Sargento was moved to the basement of the old Plymouth Post Office. In 1956 Sargento purchased the Elkhart Lake Canning Company and remodeled its 40,000 square feet into a modern packaging facility.

Packaged shredded cheeses were first introduced in 1958 and successfully marketed by Sargento, fulfilling the consumers' need for convenience and creating a whole new market.

In August 1963 Gentine began another operation in a newly constructed building in the Plymouth Industrial Park. The cheese-wrapping operation was the first in the United States to specifically package private-label, random-

The Plymouth Cheese Counter, founded by Leonard A. Gentine, was located in a small carriage house in Plymouth, Wisconsin. A mail-order gift shop and retail cheese store, it specialized in convenient, individually wrapped cheese products from Wisconsin and the world, and was the predecessor of Sargento Incorporated, a holding company with Sargento Cheese Company, Inc., Sargento Food Service Corporation, and Duralam Inc. as subsidiaries.

Leonard A. Gentine, Sr., chairman of the board of Sargento Incorporated and founder of Sargento Cheese Company, Inc.

weight cheeses.

In 1969 Sargento developed a breakthrough in retail dairy merchandising by introducing the Peg Bar. The Peg Bar allowed

consumer-size packages of cheese to be displayed at eye level, within the shoppers' reach, to create both customer and retailer enthusiasm. The results—Sargento's sales rose significantly, and the Peg Bar went on to become an industry standard. With established trade contracts and a national network of food brokers, Sargento was able to install the Peg Bar merchandiser nationwide and market new products such as shredded cheese with taco seasoning and crumbled blue cheese.

The 1970s were formative years for the company, when Sargento built a national reputation for service and quality. Sargento outgrew its production facility in 1971, and an addition was constructed at the Plymouth facility. This expansion enabled the firm to move the majority of its cheese packaging to Plymouth, permitting the Elkhart Lake facility to concentrate on the production of specialty cheese products.

In 1980 Sargento acquired a cheese-manufacturing plant in the town of Mitchell. This acquisition allowed Sargento to produce its own Italian cheeses, which strengthened its position in the marketplace and complemented its packaging operation. It was also at this time that Sargento recognized an opportunity to diversify by acquiring Duralam, Inc., of Appleton, a producer of flexible packaging film.

To better serve the food-service industry, Sargento formed Sargento Food Service Corp. in 1984. This operation supplies distributors, food processors, and other nonretail users of cheese. Late in 1986 the company reorganized and established Sargento Incorporated, a holding company, with Sargento Cheese Company, Sargento Food Service Corp., and

Duralam as subsidiaries.

At the same time Sargento Cheese introduced a new packaging innovation in order to distinguish itself in the marketplace and promote its quality image. After years of product research, the firm began using a resealable package for its shredded and fancy shredded cheese products. Similar to a ZIPLOC® plastic bag, this resealable package allows consumers to store any unused portion of cheese in the same package it was purchased in, enhancing the convenience of the product.

As a further commitment to growth and innovation, Sargento is continuously expanding its marketing and new product development staffs.

Sargento thrives on innovation, as is exhibited by its many industry firsts, which include the development and marketing of prepackaged, consumer-size Italian cheeses, convenient shredded cheeses, the retail dairy Peg Bar merchandising system, shredded seasoned taco cheese, crumbled

A selection of Sargento Cheese Company, Inc., shredded and sliced products, displayed on a Peg Bar similar to those found in retail supermarket dairy cases across America.

blue cheese, fancy shredded cheeses, and resealable packaging for its line of shredded cheeses.

Today modern, automated equipment and computer-aided operations help to ensure the efficiency of Sargento's plants. But people working together as a team is what makes it happen. The firm's skilled, dedicated work force takes pride in its work, greatly contributing to the success of the company. Sargento employees work together in a wide variety of occupations, from administrative and executive, to sales, purchasing, plant operations, and more.

Effective leadership and the cooperation of the Sargento family of employees have made Sargento Incorporated what it is today—a family company that is one of America's leading marketers of fine quality products.

WATRY INDUSTRIES, INC.

Watry Industries, Inc., was founded by Nick J. Watry in 1955. The company's first production facility was located in Campbellsport, Wisconsin. A second building was purchased in December of that year that housed the firm's offices and a small tool and die shop.

The current chairman of the board of directors, Emelyne Watry, joined the company in early 1956 as bookkeeper and receptionist. In March 1957 the firm was incorporated as Watry Industries, Inc., and its current president and chief executive officer, Earl D. Hammett, became its first full-time sales representative. The corporation's first customers were Oil Rite Corp., the Barton Co., Speed Queen Washing Machine, and International Harvester.

By 1959 business had increased to a point where it was necessary to search for a new location that would allow the company to expand its manufacturing operations. A group of businessmen from Sheboygan (including Clarence Weber, then president of Security First National Bank) were instrumental in persuading Watry Industries to purchase land on the south side of Sheboygan at 3312 Lakeshore Drive. Construction of the 20,000-square-foot facility started in the autumn of 1959

Ground breaking for the 1976 expansion of Watry Industries was attended by (right to left) Mrs. E.O. Watry, president, Watry Realty; Earl D. Hammett, president, Watry Industries; Nick J. Watry, board chairman, Watry Industries; Joseph Schilder, president, Security First National Bank; and James Kummer, general manager, Badger Structures, contractor for project.

and was completed by the following spring.

With its move to Sheboygan, Watry Industries gained a larger, more skilled work force (of 20 employees), and a much needed natural gas supplier. The company today, after five expansions, produces permanent mold aluminum castings in a 200,000-square-foot facility that now employs approximately 125 skilled and semiskilled workers.

Watry Industries has, from its inception, been an innovator in the permanent mold aluminum castings industry. The corporation's founder, Nick J. Watry, upon graduating from Marquette University in 1929, was one of the first to produce and design for this casting process. The company, under Nick Watry's direction, was also one of the first to design and build not only its casting dies, but also its operating equipment, melting furnaces, and supporting machinery.

In 1962 Watry Industries used industrial robots of its own design to automate the permanent mold casting process, relieving its work force of some of the more disagreeable tasks associated with the foundry industry.

Current president Earl D. Hammett has built on this innovative characteristic, and Watry Industries' vice-president and general manager, Michael F. Hammett, has been responsible for incorporating many state-of-the-art manufacturing concepts. Among them are statistical quality control, CAD-CAM design, CNC machining, as well as computer control sequencing of the manufacturing processes.

Today Watry Industries, Inc., designs and produces castings for many of the nation's largest companies. Among its current customers are Ford Motor Company, McGraw-Edison, Eaton Corp., Copeland Corporation, and Kohler Company.

Quality and innovation are the hallmarks that have guided this third-generation corporation to more than 30 years of expanding services to its customers and the community.

Watry Industries' original building as it appeared in 1960.

BEMIS MANUFACTURING COMPANY

The Bemis Manufacturing Company of Sheboygan Falls got its start in 1899 as the White Wagon Works. Otis Trowbridge ran the firm until his death in 1917; his son, Walter Trowbridge, then took over the direction of the company.

In 1924 Trowbridge's cousin, Albert Bemis, and George Riddell bought interest in the business and changed its name to White Coaster Wagon Works. In those early times the White Coaster Wagon Works made wooden coaster wagons and sleds. When metal-stamped wagons replaced the wooden wagons, the firm diversified its product line, adding such novelty furniture as end tables, coffee tables, magazine racks, and pipe stands.

When the Depression hit in 1932, causing sales and employment to decrease, Albert Bemis contacted A. Carl Jensen, who was with the Crocker Chair Company, which was going bankrupt, and asked Jensen to join the White Coaster Wagon Works. Jensen agreed, and brought with him toilet seat machinery, trademarks, and patents.

Over the years the employees of White Coaster Wagon Works became so skilled in all phases of the lamination, routing, sanding, and painting of toilet seats that toilet seats became the company's most fashionable product.

In 1938 the White Coaster Wagon Works became Bemis Manufacturing Company.

During the 1950s Bemis began using wood waste (sawdust), mixing it with phenolic resin and baking it under pressure to form a solid core of molded wood in its toilet seats instead of pieces of wood glued together. In 1960 Bemis entered the plastic age when it acquired an injection-molding press to mold plastic toilet seats.

Now its Injection Molding Plastic Division is one of the largest in the Upper Midwest.

Through internal growth and acquisition of other companies Bemis has become one of the largest toilet seat manufacturers in the country. One such purchase was the Church Seat Company, which Bemis moved to Sheboygan Falls in 1985 where it now continues to

make and sell "The Best Seat in the House."

Toilet seats have been the foundation for expansion into other areas. In 1971 Bemis Health Care Corporation was started to manufacture and market plastic health care items. In 1984 Bemis acquired the West Bend Humidifier Division.

Today Bemis Manufacturing Company is the second-largest employer in Sheboygan County with 1,000 employees. With the addi-

tion of the English division, Harrison-Cavalier, in 1987, Bemis currently has 10 divisions: Bemis Seats, Mayfair Seats, Church Seats, Colonial Kitchen, Tommer Knives, Bemis Contract Division, Rain Master Plastic Gutter & Downspouts, Bemis Health Care, and the Bemis Humidifier Division.

Bemis Manufacturing Com-

The dark building (center) housed the White Wagon Works, manufacturer of wooden coaster wagons and sleds. Located in Sheboygan Falls, it was founded in 1899 and was the predecessor of Bemis Manufacturing Company.

pany's product quality, coupled with its conscientious work force, have allowed it to win numerous product awards, including the Governor's Export Award in 1985 and 1986, and the Governor's New Product Award in 1986 and 1987.

PLASTICS ENGINEERING COMPANY

The history of Plastics Engineering Company reflects the technological progress of American industry over the years. From a small firm, it has become a multicomplex operation and a recognized world leader in the development and refinement of thermosetting resins and molding compounds.

The inspiration and backing for this enterprise came from the company's founder, the late Frank G. Brotz, Sr., of Kohler, Wisconsin. Brotz took a personal and active interest in the establishment and operation of the fledgling firm. Together with his five sons, he formed the American Molded Products Company, a family partnership, which began operations in Chicago on April 25, 1934. It manufactured thermosetting liquid resins and, from them, cast molded products that included handles, knobs, radio cabinets, and similar items.

Frank G. Brotz, being a man of considerable foresight, realized the significance of these synthetic materials of construction. They were proving to play a more important role in the production of individual components that required the combined properties of good electrical insulation, heat, water, and wear resistance.

In August 1934 the plant was moved to Sheboygan and its name was changed to Plastics Engineering Company. After a year the production of liquid resins and castings was discontinued in favor of pressed moldings from dry, granular molding compounds. These compounds were developed essentially from creosol-formaldehyde resins and mixed with dry fibrous and mineral fillers.

The company requirements for molding compounds were relatively small in those days and economically their production was not justified. During the fall of 1939 the partnership decided to concentrate its efforts and limited capital exclusively for a time on the development of its custom molding department. Many items were molded and finished for the utensil industry.

By 1943 some 200 workers were employed, molding and finishing phenolic components for the Army, Navy, and Air Force ordnance departments in connection with the war effort. During the war years the firm molded "flangible" bullets, which were used in the training of aerial gunners. Besides the bullets, Plastics Engineering also produced numerous electrical parts such as cable connectors, switch bases, flying suit connectors, earphone bases, and electric brake connectors.

After the war, first an acute and then a prolonged national

shortage of molding compounds developed. The company's allocations from the various producers totaled only 20,000 pounds per month.

In order for the firm to survive, the partnership decided in March 1946 to revive its manufacture of molding compounds, this time from phenol-formaldehyde resins. An addition to the Geele Avenue plant was built for this purpose and became operational in November 1946. Initially it was intended to manufacture phenolic molding compounds for company requirements only.

In November 1946 E.H. Beach joined the firm and his energy and talents were focused on the manufacturing of phenolic molding material. Markets for molding compounds and resins other than for company requirements were subsequently developed.

The molding compound manufacturing division expanded when the resin plant on North Avenue was built in 1950. In 1959 production of melamine and melamine-phenolic resins and molding compounds was initiated.

The firm grew rapidly during the 1960s and 1970s, with nine major building expansions made to the resin and molding material manufacturing plant.

A warehouse complex was constructed in 1969 and expanded in 1976. This facility enhanced the company's renowned ability to rapidly respond to customer orders and to efficiently manage its raw material and finished goods inventories. On December 1, 1973, the firm officially opened the doors to a new and distinctive general office at the corner of Eisner Avenue and Lakeshore Road.

Today Plastics Engineering Company, often known by its trade name, PLENCO, remains a closed family corporation that spans three generations. It furnishes industry with a wide range of ready-made or custom-formulated molding compounds, industrial resins, and molded products. PLENCO maintains its modern production, research, testing, and administrative facilities in Sheboygan and is represented by a fully staffed technical sales network.

Plastics Engineering Company's North 15th Street manufacturing plant spans the forefront of the photograph and encompasses industrial resin and phenolic, melamine-phenolic and polyester compound manufacturing. The 216,000-square-foot Eisner Avenue warehouse and distribution center can be seen. PLENCO's distinctive general office is located just east (right) of the warehouse.

THE VOLLRATH COMPANY

For present-day Sheboygan and its surrounding countryside, the mid-1830s were years of extraordinary significance.

In America, in Wisconsin, a cluster of frontier dwellings at the mouth of the Sheboygan River was shaping itself into a community. During those same years, in Germany, in the tiny Rhineland village of Dorrebach, a sturdy young German, Jacob Johann Vollrath, was hard at work learning the iron-molding trade. Sheboygan and Jacob Vollrath, however, did not come together until 1853, the year in which Sheboygan was chartered as a city.

When 29-year-old Jacob Vollrath, married and the father of four, brought his young family to Sheboygan, the city had no paved streets, and its permanent population numbered scarcely more than 2,000. Yet that year some 13,000 immigrants—German, Dutch, Belgian, all eager to settle Wisconsin's fertile countryside—passed across the city's docks. Most of the newcomers moved on to set up farms and households inland. Jacob Vollrath, however, saw his future in Sheboygan. Since the day of his arrival, the history of the city and the fortunes of Jacob Vollrath and his descendants have been inextricably intertwined.

Active and ambitious, Jacob Vollrath was a participant in a number of Sheboygan's pioneer business ventures. During his early years in the city he was involved in enterprises that made farm implements, built steam engines, and turned out cast-iron ranges and cooking utensils.

By 1870 the growing city was establishing itself as a center of di-

Jacob J. Vollrath, founder and first president.

versified manufacturing, and Jacob Vollrath had established himself as one of its respected business leaders, becoming a principal in the Union Steel and Iron Foundry at Ninth Street and St. Clair Avenue. By 1870 Sheboygan had discovered its civic purpose, and Jacob Vollrath had given some polish to his entrepreneurial skills.

Three years later Jacob Vollrath conveyed a substantial inter-

est in Union Steel and Iron to his son-in-law, John Michael Kohler, thus setting the stage for the development of two outstandingly successful business ventures, both of which were to bring national and international renown to Sheboygan and its neighboring communities.

With John Michael Kohler firmly established at Ninth and St. Clair, Jacob turned his attention to yet another task. In Germany, in those days, porcelain enamelware—pots, pans, pitchers, plates, cups, and bowls—produced by coating cast-iron shapes with a fired-on ceramic glaze, was common. In the United States, however, such utensils were hard to come by. Jacob Vollrath was determined to bring the porcelain enamel process to the United States and to introduce the product—tough, durable, and inexpensive—to what he correctly reasoned was an eager and insatiable market.

Characteristically, Jacob's plan was simple and direct. His 23-year-old son, Andrew, a knowledgeable foundryman, fluent in German, was to be dispatched to Europe. Andrew's mission was to make

By the mid-1890s Vollrath was already a major Sheboygan-area employer.

The first Vollrath plant and an early view of the present facility.

The Vollrath teakettle was a familiar Sheboygan landmark for many years.

himself an expert in porcelain enamel and to bring its secrets back to Sheboygan. At home, his father was to look for a location for the new operation. The Union Steel and Iron facility was to be left in John Michael Kohler's care.

By 1874 Jacob had constructed the new plant. Located at Fifth Street and Michigan, it was set up as the Sheboygan Cast Steel Co. It would do general foundry work while the porcelain enamel operation was being developed.

By 1876, with Andrew back from a second mission, production of enamelware was under way. Sold at first from the back of a wagon, sometimes driven by Jacob himself, to housewives, restaurant cooks, and a few farseeing general store operators, Vollrath enamelware soon became the new company's major product line, and the demand for Vollrath enamelware utensils quickly required additional production facilities.

Reorganized in 1884 as the Jacob J. Vollrath Manufacturing Company, the firm issued its first stock and enjoyed continued suc-

cess. Before the end of the decade the name "Vollrath" had been stamped or cast into the bottom of hundreds of thousands of quality pots and kettles, and the fame of the company and the name of its hometown had begun to spread into remote corners of the nation.

Originally intended for the domestic market, Vollrath porcelain enamelware—sturdy, durable, and easily cleaned—was quickly accepted for use in both restaurants and institutions. Hospital and health care applications soon followed. Well before the turn of the century, the company numbered many of the nation's foremost restaurants, institutions, and hospitals among its customers.

Jacob Vollrath died in 1898. He had lived long enough to see his family name and the name of the city that had been his home joined in an internationally recognized trademark. He had also lived long enough to see son-in-law John Michael Kohler well along to success, and to see his outgoing second daughter, Minnie, become John Michael's second wife. Jacob's oldest daughter Lillie, John Michael's first wife, had died in 1883, leaving behind six children. One of her sons, Walter, Ja-

cob's grandson, was to become governor of Wisconsin (1929-1931). Walter, in turn, was to have a son, Walter Jr., who would one day become a Vollrath Company president and later also serve as governor of Wisconsin (1953-1957).

Reorganizing once again after Jacob Vollrath's death, the company, under the succeeding presidency of Jacob's sons, first Andrew (1899-1907) and then Carl (1907-1932), continued to flourish. Keeping faith with their father, the younger Vollraths expanded product lines, developed new markets, and augmented production facilities. In 1910 the company, by that time simply known as The Vollrath Company, began construction of its present plant at 18th Street and Michigan Avenue. In the years that followed warehouses and branch offices were established in New York and Chicago, and distribution of Vollrath products was extended to the

West Coast.

After World War I The Vollrath Company continued to accept new challenges. New technologies were probed. There were experiments with new materials and new methods of manufacture. There were more new products and a still broader marketing range. By 1932, when J.C. Vollrath, Carl Vollrath's son, took over the company's helm, both its health care and food service functions were important forces in their respective markets.

Under J.C. Vollrath, the company steadfastly preserved its entrepreneurial traditions. Always responsive to the marketplace, Vollrath worked to turn the adversities of the 1930s into opportunities, insisting only that no new venture should place the firm's reputation for quality, integrity, and responsibility at risk. By the end of the 1930s, with war clouds once again on the horizon, the company was already replacing its enamelware with stainless steel.

In 1941 Vollrath, as responsive as ever, quickly converted to production for the military. During World War II the company turned out immense quantities of mess hall and hospital equipment and more than 12 million G.I. canteens.

In recognition of its efforts, the company received the coveted Army/Navy "E" Award for production achievement.

In 1947 Walter Kohler, Jr., Jacob's great-grandson, became Vollrath's fifth president. First elected to the firm's board of directors in 1940, he left soon after for service with the U.S.

Vollrath enamelware for the kitchen was a staple of the company's business until the 1940s.

Navy. Returning to Sheboygan after the war, he replaced the retiring J.C. Vollrath in the presidential chair. Although officially the company's president until 1968, his term as its chief executive was interrupted in 1951 when he took leave from Vollrath to campaign for the office of governor of Wisconsin. Elected in 1952, Walter Kohler, Jr., became the second of Jacob Vollrath's descendants to hold Wisconsin's governorship.

During Walter Kohler, Jr.'s, two terms as governor (1953-1955 and 1955-1957), day-to-day direction of corporate operations was turned over to Paul Rohling. Under Rohling's able stewardship, and after 1957, with Walter Kohler again in command, growth was steady and the company's dominance in its chosen markets was solidified.

In 1968 Walter Kohler turned over the corporate presidency to Rohling. With experienced Walter Kohler as its board chairman, and with the able and aggressive Paul Rohling at the president's desk, Vollrath was ready to meet the challenges of expansion and diversification.

In 1967 Vollrath acquired facilities for producing commercial refrigeration equipment. Today, much enlarged, Vollrath's Refrigeration Division in River Falls, Wisconsin, manufactures custom-designed controlled-environment rooms, walk-in coolers, and refrigerated storage enclosures for medical laboratory, hospital, restaurant, institutional, retail store, and warehouse applications.

A second expansion venture came in 1974, when the company entered international marketing. Not limited to doing business with

After World War II stainless steel replaced enamelware on Vollrath's production lines.

Vollrath employees still pride themselves on their craftsmanship.

The Vollrath Company and its suppliers alone, the International Division operates from offices in the United States, Canada, and Japan; serves buyers and sellers worldwide; and finds sources and purchasers for an ever-increasing variety of goods and services.

In 1976, still looking to extend its marketing range, Vollrath built its own molded-plastic production facilities in Gallaway, Tennessee. Additional production capacity was added in 1984. Development of molded-plastic capability made it possible for Vollrath to offer both stainless steel and molded-plastic wares from proprietary facilities.

Active to the last, Walter Kohler, Jr., continued as Vollrath's board chairman until his death in 1976. With his death, Paul Rohling assumed the chairmanship, and Terry J. Kohler, Walter Kohler, Jr.'s, son, took over the presidency.

Terry J. Kohler had come to The Vollrath Company in 1964 after service with the Air Force and study at Massachusetts Institute of Technology. At M.I.T. Terry Kohler had taken a graduate degree at the Sloan School of Management. Once with Vollrath, he wasted no time in putting his management expertise to work. Certain of the efficiency of the computer, Kohler became a driving force in the development of advanced in-

formation and control programs that quickly placed The Vollrath Company in the vanguard of computerized management technology. Within a few short years Terry Kohler had extensively reformed Vollrath management.

Under Terry Kohler's leadership, Vollrath functions were decentralized. The company's Food Service, Health Care, Refrigeration, and International divisions were restructured under divisional presidents, and its Information Services operation was elevated to full divisional status.

In 1984, in yet another reflection of his great-great-grandfather's entrepreneurial spirit, Terry Kohler directed The Vollrath Company's acquisition of North Sails, the world's largest and most technologically advanced sailmaker. With operations in 25 countries, North Sails designs and fabricates sails used in yacht racing, performance cruising, and windsurfing.

Today, from Vollrath headquarters on North 18th Street, Terry J. Kohler, chairman of the board and chief executive officer since 1982, and Ken Benson, corporate president and chief operating officer since 1985, direct the activities of a mini-conglomerate that

provides an astonishing variety of goods and services to every part of the world. Stock pots, salad bars, hospital reusables and disposables, deep-drawn stainless shapes, low-alloy precision castings, import-export marketing services, doors and panels for room-size refrigerated spaces, and jibs and spinnakers for America's Cup contenders—all are available from The Vollrath Company.

In Jacob Vollrath's time, the name "Vollrath" and the words "Made in Sheboygan" were accepted as symbols of quality in every midwestern household. Today the name "Vollrath" is an internationally recognized certification of excellence, and products bearing Vollrath trademarks are familiar worldwide.

It is now more than 125 years since an ambitious young iron molder, not long from Germany, speaking with an accent he would never lose, arrived in a promising small city on the Lake Michigan shore. Jacob Vollrath and Sheboygan grew to maturity together. Today The Vollrath Company and Sheboygan are still together.

North Sails is the newest member of the Vollrath family of companies.

RICHARDSON INDUSTRIES, INC.

Richardson Industries, Inc., a sixth-generation family affair, has undergone innumerable changes since its inception in 1848 as a sawmill.

Its stay began when Joseph E. and Carolyn Richardson, with their growing family, arrived in Sheboygan Falls in 1845 to farm. The 200 acres they purchased along the Mullet River was covered with so much virgin timber that the land had to be cleared before it could be farmed.

There were at least two dozen families in the village at that time, and there was a primitive sawmill. The mill was built in 1836 to process lumber purchased from the neighboring farmers as they cleared their land. It was at this time that Richardson made a decision to build his own mill and market the logs he cleared from his land by using the Mullet River as a source of power.

With the assistance of his wife's brother, Egbert Burhan, Richardson strategically diverted the Mullet River by building a dam above the site he selected for his mill. Upon the completion of the mill, Richardson and Burhan began sawing logs from Richardson's land, founding the J. Richardson Co.

Of the 13 children of Joseph and Carolyn, only the three oldest sons, Jairus, Egbert, and William, helped their father run the mill in

the 1850s. Over the years the sons gradually took complete charge of the mill, enabling their father to return to farming. In 1858 the brothers began to expand their operation, adding a lath mill.

When the three older brothers marched off to fight in the Civil War in 1861, their father, with the help of another son, Edward, kept the business going. During the war the brothers sent most of their paychecks home for their father to bank. When two of the brothers—Jairus was killed in the conflict—returned home three years later, they were able to use the capital that had accumulated from their savings to buy interest in the sawmill. A year later the name of the company was changed to J. Richardson & Sons.

With the timber on the original acreage nearly depleted, the broth-

This company photo, taken in 1891, shows a crew numbering more than 40 hands. Richardson Brothers Company, in its 43rd year, was engaged in custom sawmill and lumber operations.

ers purchased additional land farther up the Sheboygan River. As the business grew the mill was remodeled in 1870. A planing mill was added, and the simple paddle wheel was replaced with two turbine water wheels. Also during this time the mill business was separated into a manufacturing and a retail lumberyard division. Six years later the brothers completely bought out their father's interest and changed the name of the business to Richardson Brothers.

The next major addition to the business came in 1881, when the crafting of chairs was added to the manufacturing division. This

Richco Structures, Haven.

Richardson Brothers Company, Sheboygan Falls.

new line came about when a brawl in a local saloon one night resulted in every chair in the place being broken. The following day the saloonkeeper asked the Richardson brothers to find a chair that could "really take it." Apparently the chair that the brothers designed, which was heavy, round-backed, and reinforced at weak points by iron rods, was to the saloonkeeper's satisfaction; he ordered enough to replace all of his broken chairs.

Edward Richardson sold out his interest in the business and headed west. In 1891 Egbert Richardson met with an unfortunate accident as he and a crew of men, shortly after the ice in the Sheboygan River had thawed, went to Millhome to drive lumber they had logged during the winter down the river to the mill. The logs were piled in high places on the river bank with each pile held in place by a key log. When the key log was released, the pile of logs would fall into the river and float downstream. Someone accidentally released the key log on a pile before Egbert could step clear, and he became trapped in the rolling logs, ending up in the icy water. Egbert survived, but was so badly injured that he died a year later at the age of 51. His father, at 80 years of age, died the

following year.

William, as the sole remaining Richardson brother, ran the family business. Egbert's son Joseph (also known as Egbert) entered the business in 1899, engaging in the lumberyard and sawmill operation. William's sons, Jairus and Lemont, became involved in the manufacturing end of the operation in the 1900s.

Under third-generation management Richardson interests expanded in both furniture manufacturing and the building supply business. Then, in 1925, William Richardson died.

Ten years later Jairus turned from the manufacture of furniture to the design and manufacture of woodworking machinery, and formed a new and distinct or-

Richardson Lumber Company East, Sheboygan.

ganization known today as the J.S. Richardson Company. Of Jairus Richardson's two sons, William and John, William stayed with the furniture enterprise and became president, while John joined his father's machinery company. During this same period Egbert was joined in the lumberyard and sawmill operations of the Richardson Brothers Company by his son, Joseph E.

As the business flourished father and son added a retail lumber outlet in 1936 and named it the Richardson Lumber Company. Two years later a wholesale lumber and building materials distribution operation known as Falls Dealer Supply was founded, with Joseph E. as president of both entities.

Up until that point the Richardson sawmill, lumberyard, and furniture-manufacturing operations were all headquartered on the original 1848 site. The J.S. Richardson Company had been established at another location.

In 1946 Joseph E., a fourth-generation member of the family, incorporated each of the new Richardson enterprises and moved the lumber company and Falls Dealer Supply from the landmark site to the present location on Highway 28 in Sheboygan Falls.

The next decade saw Joseph E. Richardson's three sons—Joseph Jr., Charles, and David—becoming the fifth generation to actively engage in the family business. In 1961 the senior Joseph Richardson and his sons bought out the furniture company interests from other members of the Richardson Brothers Company.

In 1973 Richardson Industries, Inc., was formed. Richardson Lumber Company and Falls Dealer Supply became divisions of the organization. Richardson Brothers remained a separate corporation until 1979, when it also

Richardson Lumber Company West, Sheboygan Falls.

Richardson Furniture Emporium, Sheboygan Falls.

was merged into Richardson Industries, Inc.

The resulting corporation is organized into six manufacturing and sales divisions.

Richardson Brothers Company, Sheboygan Falls (employing 400), manufactures award-winning solid wood dining room furniture that is sold nationally and in Canada. Showrooms are maintained in High Point, North Carolina; Minneapolis, Minnesota; Dallas, Texas; Atlanta, Georgia; and San Francisco, California.

Richardson Lumber Company, Sheboygan Falls and Sheboygan (employing 40), is one of the largest retail building material yards in Wisconsin. It offers complete building services for do-it-yourselfers and contractors.

Richco Structures, Sheboygan Falls, Haven, and Green Bay (employing 120), manufactures roof and floor trusses that are sold throughout the Midwest to lumberyards and contractors. It is recognized as the leading wooden truss manufacturer in Wisconsin.

Menominee Lumber Company, Menominee, Minnesota (employing 45), manufactures hard-

wood moulding and stair parts, selling them nationwide.

Green Bay Wood Preserving, Green Bay (employing 10), produces chemically treated "green wood" that resists rot and moisture. It is distributed throughout Wisconsin and Upper Michigan.

Richardson Furniture Emporium and Gift Gallery, Sheboygan Falls, is a retail furniture and gift store specializing in solid oak furniture and accessories.

Officers of Richardson Industries are chairman David Richardson; president Joseph Richardson, Jr.; vice-presidents, Evelyn Richardson, Marvin Debbink, Glen Dulmes, and Joseph Richardson III (sixth-generation family member); and secretary/treasurer Gerald Loth.

Richardson Industries, Inc., has clearly identified its mission. It is a group of businesses devoted to servicing both homes and commercial buildings. This includes planning, building, and furnishing them, both inside and out. With this mission clearly in mind, the company is ready to continue into the twenty-first century, experiencing new opportunities for further growth and expansion.

SHEBOYGAN PAINT COMPANY

The Sheboygan Paint Company was started as a copartnership by William A. Knilans and E.S. Wheeler in 1921 under the name of Knilans-Wheeler Varnish Company. A year later Stuart C. Knilans joined his father in the business. On June 22, 1923, Knilans-Wheeler Varnish Company's name was changed to the Sheboygan Paint Company upon its incorporation. The charter provided for the buying and selling of paint, varnish, and other merchandise in the firm's first production facility at the corner of Eighth Street and Erie Avenue.

In 1930 land for a permanent factory was purchased from the American Chair Company on North Water Street, and a new plant was built. The early 1930s were trying times for all businesses, including the Sheboygan Paint Company. It was only through the efforts of the Citizens' State Bank and the cooperation of many raw material suppliers and other creditors that the firm survived.

During the late 1930s and throughout the 1940s the company went from marginal profitability to moderate profitability. Progress of the corporation was limited due to lack of technical and manufacturing expertise. Irvin F. Eder was brought into the firm in 1951 as chief chemist and general manager. His broad background in technical and production areas enabled the organization to compete with other paint companies. That same year Eder acquired a proprietary position in the corporation and in 1958 became co-owner with Stuart C. Knilans.

John P. Brownrigg, stepson of Stuart C. Knilans, joined the firm in 1952 and soon became knowledgeable in all areas of the paint

William A. Knilans, founder.

business. Two years later John L. Nelesen came to the Sheboygan Paint Company as a laboratory technician. He was primarily concerned with customer service and selling until 1977, when Eder disposed of his interest in the corporation to Nelesen and Brownrigg.

Over the next three years the Sheboygan Paint Company experienced steady progress, and the firm was able to purchase 5.5 acres from the city of Sheboygan on Superior Avenue between 23rd and 25th streets and build a warehouse on the site. In 1961 an office

and another warehouse were added, followed by a new factory in 1966.

Brock Brownrigg, son of John, joined the company as a laboratory technician in 1977, working chiefly in the area of materials management. Two years later Larry W. Weidig started working at the firm as a comptroller and office manager.

In 1961 a subsidiary, Inland Realty Corporation, was formed in Sheboygan. Thirteen years later a retail store to service the home owner was opened on 15th Street and Superior Avenue. In 1984 a similar store opened in Green Bay, Wisconsin, and another subsidiary, Sheboygan Paint Company,

The Sheboygan facility of Sheboygan Paint Company where 90 people are employed. The firm's work force includes another 20 people at its Cedartown plant.

of Cedartown, Georgia, was formed.

Today 90 people are employed at the Sheboygan location in a 45,000-square-foot plant, and 20 people work at the Cedartown plant in a 15,000-square-foot facility.

Present officers of the Sheboygan Paint Company are John P. Brownrigg, president and treasurer; John L. Nelesen, vice-president and general manager; Brock L. Brownrigg, secretary; and Larry W. Weidg, comptroller.

FIRST INTERSTATE CORPORATION OF WISCONSIN

First Interstate Corporation of Wisconsin is growing on a strong foundation established in the 1800s by two Sheboygan banks, merged in 1957 as Citizens Bank of Sheboygan. Today it is a statewide bank holding company distinguished for its service to customers and to communities.

Its earliest forerunners were a small private bank formed in 1855, two years after the birth of the City of Sheboygan, and Citizens State Bank, organized in 1896 with capital stock of $40,000 and the motto "The Bank That Service Built." The private bank closed briefly after the Civil War and reopened in 1873 as the chartered First National Bank of Sheboygan (later known as the Bank of Sheboygan). The two institutions operated across the street from one another in downtown Sheboygan for 61 years.

Citizens State Bank was admitted to the Federal Reserve system in 1918, and within six years had become the second-largest bank in the state outside of Milwaukee. It established Citizens Northside Bank in Sheboygan as an affiliate in 1927. During the next nine years it acquired offices in Cedar Grove, Sheboygan Falls, and Plymouth.

The institution grew and pros-

pered through periods of boom and years of depression, and by 1941 it had become the second-largest state-chartered bank in Wisconsin, with total resources of more than $9 million. It maintained that distinction for many years, contributing substantially to Sheboygan's reputation of having the largest per-capita bank deposits of any city in Wisconsin.

Both banks had trust departments which originated in the early 1930s—a time when trust officers were among the most versatile of bank employees. In those days they did all of their accounting by hand, conducted household auctions, and sold insurance in addition to working with trust customers.

On December 31, 1957, Citizens Bank of Sheboygan and the Bank of Sheboygan merged. Through the years Citizens had developed into a commercial bank with many sizable corporate relationships, while the Bank of Sheboygan specialized in personal savings and consumer installment loans. With their complimentary services and well-established trust departments, they constituted a well-rounded banking organization.

When the institutions merged as Citizens Bank of Sheboygan, the organization moved into a new structure designed by a protege of Frank Lloyd Wright. The unique building, acclaimed as an

The original Bank of Sheboygan accepted deposits and issued its own currency in various denominations. This currency, issued in 1865, includes a three dollar bill.

architectural landmark, drew visitors from every state in the union and many foreign countries. It is now the home of First Interstate Bank of Wisconsin in Sheboygan.

Citizens Bancorporation, an outgrowth of this institution, was formed as a multibank holding company in 1969. Through acquisitions, Citizens Bancorporation rapidly expanded its banking locations into the Green Bay and Milwaukee areas, as well as into Manitowoc and Oconto counties.

The Citizens Trust Company, originally a department of the Bank of Sheboygan, was established as a subsidiary in 1979. Handling employee benefits and personal trusts, as well as a few less traditional accounts with assets such as play royalties, stamp and coin collections, and ownerships in corporations, it experienced tremendous growth.

August 14, 1984, marked a historic date for both the holding company and for midwestern banking, when Citizens Bancorporation implemented the first bank franchise agreement established east of Denver. On that date the holding company made the transition to First Interstate Corporation of Wisconsin, the result of a fran-

These teller cages stood in the lobby of the First National Bank of Sheboygan building, erected at the corner of North Eighth Street and Center Avenue in 1874.

Citizens Bancorporation announced its name change to First Interstate Corporation of Wisconsin in gala ceremonies August 14, 1984. The bank holding company's franchise agreement with First Interstate Bancorp, Los Angeles, was a historic event in the midwestern banking community.

M.H. Gibson, F.S. Rodger, Dayton F. Pauls, and O.L. Hall took part in ground-breaking ceremonies for the structure that housed the merged Bank of Sheboygan and Citizens State Bank, beginning in 1957. To reflect the consolidation, the new institution was named Citizens Bank of Sheboygan.

chise agreement with First Interstate Bancorp, a multistate banking organization headquartered in Los Angeles. The company's 24 offices became First Interstate Bank of Wisconsin, and its subsidiaries also assumed the First Interstate identity.

The agreement gave the holding company exclusive license to represent First Interstate in Wisconsin, to participate in a core of consumer services standard to First Interstate banks, and to gain access to additional products and services, capital resources, technology, and expertise. It could now offer services on a national and international scale, while retaining local ownership, management, and control.

In the 1984 annual report, the franchise arrangement between the Sheboygan-based holding company and the nation's ninth-largest banking company—a $55-billion global banking organization—was described as "the best of two worlds."

Late in 1984 the holding company purchased the Gottsacker Insurance Agency, Inc. Now First Interstate Insurance Agency of Wisconsin, it has become one of

the largest independent insurance agencies in the state. Its more than 50 employees offer a full range of traditional retail insurance products as well as an extensive annuity program.

The former discount brokerage division of the trust company became a full-service broker/dealer and an independently licensed subsidiary of the trust company in 1986, and was one of the first banking affiliates of its kind to become fully licensed. Trust company assets under management grew in excess of one million dollars in 1986, approximately the entire size of the trust company when it was formed seven years earlier.

By 1986 the trust company managed nearly $500 million in assets and had regional offices in Milwaukee, Appleton, Eau Claire, and Green Bay, as well as Sheboygan. It provides trust services to 14 nonaffiliated banks as well as to all of First Interstate's Wisconsin affiliates.

First Interstate Bank of Wisconsin's acquisition of banks in Eau Claire in 1985 and Appleton in 1986, and the addition of the five Continental Bank offices in Milwaukee in 1986, marked the holding company's expansion into the western part of the state and enhanced the corporation's presence in both the northeastern region and the metropolitan Milwaukee

area.

First Interstate Corporation is now represented in most major Wisconsin communities. Through a growing group of subsidiaries it offers a diverse range of financial services, including mortgage, leasing, and management services, and a variety of nonbank financial services, including securities brokerage, insurance, and trust. In 1987 it was the fifth-largest holding company in Wisconsin, with assets approaching $1.5 billion.

The strength of First Interstate Corporation of Wisconsin lies in its ability to provide customers with the financial services they need and want, while operating from a strong core of community banks. Through its banking offices, growing trust service, discount brokerage network, and insurance offices, the bank holding company has access to most financial services markets in the state. With a strong capital base, it has laid the groundwork to support future growth and innovation, and it is carefully positioned to take advantage of future developments in the areas of regional and national interstate banking.

BALLHORN CHAPELS, INC.

When Johann Ballhorn and his wife, Louisa, immigrated from Europe to the village of Glenbulah in Sheboygan County, he pursued his trade of cabinetmaking. In 1882 the Ballhorns made the decision to move to Sheboygan, where

When John Ballhorn died suddenly in 1932, his son, Milton, who received formal training at Worsham Mortuary School in Chicago, became proprietor of the furniture and funeral business. Over a seven-year period the furniture

The Ballhorn Furniture Store, shown here (above) in 1929, was established by Johann Ballhorn in 1882 at the corner of Eighth Street and St. Clair Avenue. Soon a funeral home was added, and over several generations of the family the facility has evolved with the addition of the East and West chapels (left) in 1957, and as it looks today (below).

they established a furniture business on Eighth Street and St. Clair Avenue.

Upon the death of Johann Ballhorn in 1899, the couple's son, John, continued the furniture business with undertaking as a specialty. In the early 1900s a new store was built next to the old one, and a new truck ushered in the era of motorized delivery vehicles for the firm.

It was during the Civil War that embalming, as we know it today, was pioneered. This temporary preservation of human remains allowed the bodies of soldiers to be returned home for burial. During that time, and up until the 1920s, most embalming and funeral ceremonies were done in the deceased person's home.

During the Roaring '20s the introduction of buildings designed specifically for funeral purposes came into existence. In the late 1920s John and his wife, Lillie, implemented construction of the Ballhorn Funeral Temple. The new facility was equipped with an embalming room, reposing rooms, offices, and living quarters for the director.

storefront was modernized and the funeral temple expanded. This expansion, which created the East and West chapels, also caused the name to be changed to Ballhorn Chapels.

In 1955, after graduating from the Wisconsin Institute of Mortuary Science, John Ballhorn III, son of Milton and Hildegarde Ballhorn, became associated with the family business as an embalmer and funeral director. Two years later, due to the growth of the business, the Ballhorn Chapels again expanded, providing more parking space. The main floor of the furniture store was transformed into a chapel and designated the North Chapel. With three chapels, each supplying private family rooms with a separate

exit to parking, three services and visitations could be held at the same time.

In 1947 Milton Ballhorn effected construction of the first crematory located in a funeral establishment in the State of Wisconsin. Shortly after the death of Milton Ballhorn in 1962, the furniture business was closed.

In 1967 John Ballhorn III became president of Ballhorn Chapels, Inc. Since then building additions and improvements have resulted in the Ballhorn Chapels currently occupying one-quarter of a city block.

Today Ballhorn Chapels, Inc., which is in its fourth generation of family involvement over a 106-year period, is still serving the Sheboygan County area.

AMETEK, INC.
PLYMOUTH PRODUCTS DIVISION

The forerunner to the Plymouth Products Division of Ametek, Inc.—Plymouth Industrial Products (PIP)—was founded in 1949 by Aldred J. Simmons. Simmons, who had been the general manager of the Plastics Division of Cleveland Container Corp., purchased the Plastics Division from Cleveland Container and named his new company Plymouth Industrial Products. The plant and office were located in Plymouth, Wisconsin.

In 1953 PIP leased space in the old Sheboygan Chair Company facility, which was located on the east end of Indiana Avenue in Sheboygan, and moved its office to this new location. The Plymouth plant also remained in operation. Both plants produced a variety of injection- and compression-molded items, including a number of custom-molded parts —primarily containers and supports as part of contracts with the military.

In May 1967 PIP was purchased by Ametek, Inc., and became the Plymouth Plastics Division of Ametek. The division name was changed to the present Plymouth Products in 1974.

As the product lines changed through the years, the government contract work diminished and eventually was eliminated by the mid-1970s. As a result of the declining government business, the Plymouth, Wisconsin, plant was closed in 1970, with the property donated to the City of Plymouth four years later.

In 1972 Ametek purchased some chair factory buildings on Fifth and Indiana Avenue. The 100-year-old structures were razed in stages and a new, modern facility erected on the site. The first large building was constructed in 1978. The second manufacturing area was erected two years later, and in 1985 the new office building was completed, giving this division approximately 148,000 square feet of manufacturing and office space.

The present general manager, Harold E. Cosson, was preceded by John H. Thornton, Sr., Thomas Baragry, Jr., and Dennis J. Goner-

The Ametek/Plymouth Products Division Sheboygan operation as it existed in 1967 when purchased by Ametek.

The Ametek/Plymouth Products Division as it appears today at Fifth and Indiana Avenue.

trial use, consisting of filter housings in a variety of sizes, replaceable cartridge elements to fit all the different sizes and in a variety of filtration media, and filtration systems to treat drinking wa-

ing, who followed Aldred Simmons. Currently the division employs approximately 150 people.

The Plymouth Products Division produces two proprietary lines of products. The first is a line of underground access boxes, consisting of curb and valve boxes, meter boxes, and control valve boxes, primarily for the water and gas industry. The second is a line of filtration devices for home and industrial use, consisting of filter ter for specific contaminants.

Ametek, Inc., the parent company, is a diversified manufacturer of scientific and industrial equipment with 26 divisions and plants located throughout the United States, as well as several foreign countries.

PEMCO COMPANY

Pemco (Packaging Equipment Manufacturing Company) had its start January 1, 1960, in a 20-square-foot room at the back of a tombstone factory. It was a two-man operation, with Fred Koehn and Lou J. Feurstein using the rented space to rebuild or customize old packaging equipment for specific purposes.

Before the end of 1960 Pemco's operations were moved to larger quarters. Within two years the firm was designing and building its own Pemcomatic packaging machines. The company's first machine, a Pemcomatic Model 55, which wrapped folio-size reams of paper, was sold to the Wausau Paper Mills Company in 1962. Eventually Pemco sold other custom-built machinery to major U.S. companies, as well as exported machinery to firms in England, France, Germany, and other foreign countries. As a result of Pemco's growth, and with export sales increasing, the company responded to a need for a high-speed packaging system that reduced labor costs and increased

Pemco Company's new building at 3333 Crocker Avenue in the Sheboygan Industrial Park.

productivity in the paper industry. As a result of this innovative foresight, the firm now designs and builds complete packaging systems that assemble products of specific quantities and size, wrap or box them, label them, put them into a shipping carton, seal the carton, and place them on pallets. In 1981 Pemco Company was purchased by E.C.H. Will GmbH and Company of Hamburg, Germany. Pemco and the Will organization had a "natural coming together" due to a close business relationship between the two companies that had developed years before. From its humble beginnings Pemco Company had grown into a major Sheboygan employer, with its 200 employees housed in a modern 100,000-square-foot plant in the Sheboygan Industrial Park. The firm attributes its growth and success to a good

Pemco Company is an employee-oriented organization. Here some of its 200 employees help to commemorate the 25th anniversary of the packaging systems manufacturer.

employee/family atmosphere. At Pemco, employees have paid vacations, profit sharing, health and dental insurance, and company picnics and parties. Every six months Pemco's management team meets with the employees to discuss where the company is and where it is going, air constructive criticism, and vote on matters affecting the workers and their families. In addition to being people oriented, Pemco is also product quality oriented; over the past seven years it has continuously aspired to improve its research department and develop new equipment. As a result of Pemco manufacturing some of the world's finest automatic packaging equipment and custom-built machinery, it received the Army/Navy "E" Award from the U.S. Department of Commerce in 1976 for its efforts and innovation in exporting. The firm also received the presidential "E" Star Award for exporting excellence in 1982, becoming one of only a dozen Wisconsin firms to earn that honor. As to the future, Pemco Company envisions expansion and continued success for its industry and its equipment, where technically the company will endeavor to lead and dominate the industry.

THE SCHWARZ FISH COMPANY

The Schwarz Brothers Fish Company of Sheboygan was founded in 1911 by Herman Schwarz, Sr., and his brother, William Schwarz. When the business began it employed just two men who worked in a building the size of a two-car garage.

In 1922 a smokehouse, cold storage, and freezer were constructed on the Schwarz property. Two years later Herman Schwarz bought out his brother's interest in the firm and changed its name to H.C. Schwarz Fish Company.

In 1926, in order to make room for a warehouse and a terminal for the West Port Steamship Company, the H.C. Schwarz Fish Company was forced by the city to tear down the smokehouse and its buildings along the Sheboygan River. New smokehouses were then constructed on Herman Schwarz' south Ninth Street property. As the business grew, Herman Schwarz expanded into the handling of shrimp, lobster tails, seafood, and other varieties of fish.

A Kissel chassis truck, purchased in 1926, contained a divided compartment with an insulated metal bin that held fresh fish in the front section, and smoked fish and other items in the rear section. Paul Krueger, a Sheboygan carriage maker, structured the streamlined panel body on the Kissel chassis that Herman Schwarz,

Herman Schwarz, president and chairman.

Sr., designed. It was purported to be the first streamlined panel truck in the United States.

In 1938 Marcel Schwarz, son of Herman Schwarz, Sr., acquired the business and changed the name to The Schwarz Fish Company, which incorporated in 1946. The firm's retail fish market, opened in 1953 on South Franklin Street, was managed by Herman Schawarz, Sr.'s, niece, Marcella Thrill Gross.

In addition to the filleting of fresh-water fish and commercial smoking, the organization has been custom smoking trout and salmon for sports fishermen. In 1975 more than 3 million pounds of fish were handled, ranking The Schwarz Fish Company as one of the largest fish companies in Wisconsin.

Today the fish plant, under its fourth generation of family ownership, receives fresh-water fish from all five of the Great Lakes, plus many Canadian lakes. The Schwarz Fish Company employs 36 people, including the retail fish market, and has a fleet of vehicles consisting of three large refrigerated trucks, a panel truck, and two automobiles for the sales department personnel.

In addition to the refrigerators at the company's Ninth Street plant, there is a freezer at Mrs. Marcel Schwarz' property that holds 100,000 pounds of fish. At varying times the firm has housed a total of 500,000 pounds of fish that was stored in various freezers in Milwaukee, Green Bay, and Canada.

The corporate officers of The Schwarz Fish Company are Herman Schwarz, president and chairman of the board; Mrs. Marcel Schwarz, vice-president; Neil Schwarz, secretary; and Noreen Schwarz Courtright, treasurer.

The current plant on 3028 South Ninth Street with the fleet of company vehicles (below) contrasted with the H.C. Schwarz Fish Company's first 1926 paneled Kissel chassis truck (inset).

FIRST WISCONSIN NATIONAL BANK

First Wisconsin National Bank of Sheboygan was founded by John Ewing and his son-in-law, James Mead. Ewing and Mead traveled to the Midwest from Vermont searching for a place to start a bank. They chose Sheboygan, appreciating its countryside similarities to Vermont, and opened the German Bank in 1856. The institution was located on the northwest corner of Eighth and Pennsylvania Avenue. Ten years later, with George Cole as president, the bank relocated across the street from its original headquarters.

In 1873 James Mead became president. Mead not only ran the bank, but also founded the Phoenix Chair Company and was one of the organizers of the Crocker Chair Company. Mead became prominent in Sheboygan, both in business and in society. In fact, Sheboygan's public library was named after him.

In addition to banking, Mead was also the bank's travel agent for the steamship lines and the railroads. The travel agency service was a feeder for the bank in the sense that when immigrants wanted to come to Sheboygan for a job in a furniture factory or with Kohler Company, the German Bank Travel Agency would make their travel accommodations and set up a savings account for the immigrants so they could one day bring their families here to join them.

The travel agency soon became known as the first travel agency in the State of Wisconsin, and eventually became an entity of its own, even though it was still located in and owned by the bank.

In 1882 a new bank building was erected on the corner of Eighth and Commerce Street. This new facility was unique at that time because it was three stories

Security National Bank was "Sheboygan's only skyscraper" in 1923 when the bank opened.

James H. Mead, one of the founders and president of the German Bank from 1873 to 1891.

high. Nine years later, after 18 years as president of the German Bank, James Mead died. He was succeeded by Fred Karste.

A few years later the institution, after expanding to a seven-story structure, reorganizing un-

der a national charter, and being renamed Security National Bank, opened its doors to "Sheboygan's only skyscraper." William J. Rietow was president of the Security National Bank at this time.

From 1945 to the present, under the presidency of Clarence Weber, Joseph Schilder, Gerald Thorne, and David Rauwerdink, the bank's assets grew from $20 million to $280 million.

Since the turn of the century Security First National Bank has played an important role in helping to build Sheboygan into what it is today. Its Commercial Loan Department has been instrumental over the past 20 years in lending to and counseling small businesses. As a result of the bank's expertise in different government-

Founded in 1856 as the German Bank, the institution has weathered relocations and name changes to emerge as First Wisconsin National Bank.

assisted financing programs, Sheboygan County and its surrounding areas have enjoyed the success of these small businesses in the form of growth in employment, income, and tax base.

According to David A. Rauwerdink, current president of First Wisconsin National Bank of Sheboygan, "Back in the 1970s we made a commitment to revive and sustain small business activity in the community by providing a vital foundation of economic growth and stability. Through the use of government-assisted financing programs, we are providing long-term, fixed-rate financing for our area businesses' growth and expansion."

In 1983 Security First National Bank was chosen as a preferred lender by the Small Business Administration. This status was granted to only 25 banks nationwide.

Gerald M. Thorne, current chairman of the board, and Russell J. Schuler, senior vice-president and senior lending officer, were named Wisconsin Small Business Financial Advocates in 1984 and 1986.

In 1985 Security First National Bank announced its merger and the merger of its holding company, Security Financial Services, Inc. (a six-bank holding company), with First Wisconsin Corporation, the largest bank holding company in the State of Wisconsin. With this merger came a new name, First Wisconsin National Bank.

Gerald M. Thorne (left), chairman of the board, and David A. Rauwerdink, president, share a moment in overlooking downtown Sheboygan from the restaurant on top of the building.

KOHLER CO.

From a hog scalder with legs to the elegant Rapport Whirlpool Bath, Kohler Co. of Kohler, Wisconsin, has successfully grown to become the nation's leading manufacturer of plumbing and leisure products.

The Kohler name, however, is not associated exclusively with plumbing products. Power products—engines and generators—are also an integral part of the Kohler spectrum of products. In fact, the Kohler name and reputation for dependability became firmly established when Admiral Richard Byrd took five Kohler electric generators on his 1926 expedition to Antarctica to supply power to his headquarters.

Because of that successful mission, Byrd requested Kohler-made generators again when he made a second Antarctic expedition in 1933. Upon his arrival there, Byrd discovered that the first electric generators, which were left behind from his previous expedition, still worked.

The American Club in Kohler blends old-world charm with world-class accommodations. It is Wisconsin's only AAA Five-Diamond hotel and the focal point of Kohler's growing hospitality business.

Today Kohler Co. is one of the world's largest manufacturers of air-cooled, four-cycle engines and a major manufacturer of generators.

After 114 years of providing products that enhance gracious living, Kohler is now reaching out to attract visitors to its headquarters community. Under theme "Kohler Village: An American Original," are such attractions as The American Club, a historic village inn; Blackwolf Run, a Pete Dye-designed 27-hole championship golf course; Sports Core, a complete health and racquet facility; River Wildlife, a 600-acre nature preserve; the Kohler Design Center, a dazzling showcase for Kohler products; and Woodlake Market and Shops.

Located in the heart of Kohler Village, The American Club features famed restaurants, 160 luxurious guest rooms, and an elegant conference center. Built in 1918 to provide temporary housing for immigrant employees, it was closed in 1978 for extensive refurbishing. Since its grand reopening in 1981, The American Club has received many distinctive awards, including prestigious AAA Five-Diamond Awards.

Innovation and bold craftsmanship have made Kohler Co. the leader in the plumbing industry.

The newest addition to the Kohler hospitality businesses is Woodlake Market and Shops. Woodlake, a single-story brick and stone complex situated on 6.5 landscaped acres, houses a unique grocery market and a variety of specialty shops.

Other businesses of note are the Kohler Farms, where a unique strain of flavorful, low-fat, low-cholesterol Chianina beef cattle are raised, and Kohler Stables, the home of championship Morgan horses.

From the firm's humble beginnings in 1873, when Austrian immigrant John Michael Kohler purchased the Sheboygan Union Iron & Steel Foundry, Kohler Co. has grown to an international firm with 12,500 employees worldwide. With more than 5,600 people working in Wisconsin alone, the company is one of the state's largest employers. Under the leadership of Herbert V. Kohler, Jr., a grandson of the founder, it remains one of the largest privately held companies in the world.

RINDT ENTERPRISES

Rindt Enterprises is a company that was incorporated in 1977, but whose roots go back to 1919 and the J. Bensman Foods Company. That year Joe Bensman, founder of the company, began selling groceries at 2128 North 12th Street. In 1929 he opened a second store at 909 Michigan Avenue. During the next 10 years the firm expanded rapidly and was operating 10 stores. Robert Rindt began working at one of those stores in 1934. By 1940 he had been promoted to store manager.

After World War II Rindt became a partner with Joe Bensman's sons, Paul and Ben. Together they formed Bensman's

The first Park & Shop store on Erie Avenue. Photo circa 1960

Bensman's grocery store on Michigan Avenue in Sheboygan where Robert Rindt bagged groceries. Photo circa 1945

Park & Shop Inc. In 1953 they opened one of the first supermarkets in the area. Located at 1807 Erie Avenue, the store was called Park & Shop. This proved to be a very successful store. By 1961 the facility had been expanded three times to handle the ever-increasing business. A second Park & Shop store was built at 823 South Eighth Street in 1956.

At that time Sol Bensman joined the business, Ben Bensman left the company, and Joe retired. This left the operation of the two supermarkets to Paul, Bob, and Sol.

In 1965, at Paul Bensman's passing, Robert Rindt became president of both Bensman's Park & Shop and J. Bensman Foods. Seven years later Bob and Sol opened two additional Park & Shop stores—one at the Northgate Shopping Center and the other at K mart Plaza. By this time most of the older Bensman stores had

been closed or sold, and the company only operated supermarkets. During the 1970s the two newer Park & Shop stores enjoyed great success, with both facilities adding service bakery and deli departments. Sol Bensman retired in 1976 and sold out his interest in the two companies to the Rindt family. It was then that Rindt Enterprises was formed as a parent company to operate the four Park & Shop stores.

In May 1984 Rindt Enterprises opened its largest store, Park & Save Foods, located at 1317 North 25th Street. At that time the two older Park & Shop stores, on Eighth Street and on Erie Avenue, were closed. The Park & Save store has many features for the modern consumer, including a pharmacy, video rentals, deli, bakery, and self-service gasoline.

Rindt Enterprises continues to grow by adapting to customers' needs and providing quality products and services in clean, up-to-date facilities.

THE MAYLINE COMPANY

Since the late 1930s The Mayline Company of Sheboygan has built the reputation of being one of the largest manufacturers of drafting room furniture and related equipment in the United States. It is also one of the largest and most progressive firms in Sheboygan.

The Mayline Company was founded in Chicago by the late Harry L. DeLisle under the name Engineering Sales Company, using the trade name of ESCO. The firm later moved to Two Rivers, Wisconsin, where it remained until the spring of 1939. At that time ESCO needed larger quarters, due to its growth, and transferred to Eau Claire Avenue in Sheboygan.

In 1940 DeLisle died in a boating accident. According to the terms of his will, the business was to be operated under the guidance of an administrator for a period of five years.

Due to the firm's steady growth, it moved in 1944 to a larger facility at 619 North Commerce Street. Upon the company being incorporated in 1946 and purchased from the estate, Ellwood H. May became president and treasurer, Mary May became vice-president and secretary, and Harold Mais became assistant secretary and treasurer. That same

Harold H. Mais, president and chief operating officer.

year the firm added a new line of drafting products and changed its trade name and its corporate name to The Mayline Company.

Sixteen years later the former Chicago Northwestern Railway freight depot was purchased by Mayline and renovated as a shipping and receiving department. In the years that followed additional buildings were erected, with major expansions of 56,000 square feet undertaken in 1967, and 30,000 square feet in 1981.

After the death of Ellwood May in 1974, The Mayline Company was purchased by Charles L. Barancik of Northbrook, Illinois. Harold H. Mais, who has been with the company for 42 years, has been president and chief operating officer since 1975; Robert Kattner is vice-president/sales; and Joe Franzone is vice-president/manufacturing.

With the previous acquisition of the Associated Seed Growers building, The Mayline Company now has a total of 300,000 square feet of manufacturing and office space. There products of wood, steel, and plastic are designed and manufactured for architects, engineers, and designers, as well as for students.

Mais attributes the success of The Mayline Company to its 275 employees, who year after year continue to produce products of exceptionally high quality. Thanks to this reputation for quality, The Mayline Company distributes drafting furniture and equipment with accessories through 4,500 dealers throughout the United States and Canada, and through its International Sales Division.

The Mayline Company complex at 619 North Commerce Street, Sheboygan.

KIEFFER & CO., INC.

In 1959 Don Kieffer left Federal Signs in Chicago and purchased a Sheboygan sign company. Don Kieffer Signs operated predominately in the Sheboygan area as a design, sales, installation, and service company with four to six employees. Over the years Kieffer Signs operated an active highway sign business. Painted and electric signs were also sold, with some electric signs being purchased from outside vendors.

In 1978 Steve Kieffer joined his father in the sign-making business, determined to help the operation grow. When Kieffer & Co. incorporated the following year, a decision was made to expand the firm and manufacture its own products. That decision resulted in the company phasing out the painted and highway sign business and adding a sales force.

In 1982 Kieffer & Co., Inc., purchased an existing business in Illinois as a sales branch. This acquisition not only allowed the firm access to the Chicago metropolitan market, but also helped its sales to exceed one million dollars per year.

As a result of the Illinois production plant being moved to Sheboygan in 1983 and a substantial growth in Wisconsin sales, Kieffer constructed a 32,000-square-foot facility on a five-acre tract in the Sheboygan Industrial Park.

Today Kieffer & Co., Inc., built on 30 years of experience in the sign business, is a thriving manufacturer, serving regional, national, and international accounts. The firm's modern facility, encompassing 60,000 square feet and employing 70 people, with sales and service facilities in several major cities, enables it to produce quality products using the most advanced equipment and technology available.

Kieffer & Co. produces signs in all sizes for major department store chains, banks, clinics and hospitals, motels, retail chains, supermarkets, restaurants, industrial complexes, real estate developers, architectural firms, and shopping malls.

Kieffer signs are made by skilled craftsmen, knowledgeable in the many fields of expertise that go into pattern making, metal fabrication, face decorating, painting, welding, woodworking, neon tube bending, electrical wiring, and electronics. Each sign produced by Kieffer & Co., Inc., must not only meet its own strict quality-control

Skilled craftsmen give careful attention to detail in all aspects of assembly and quality control.

Kieffer & Co., Inc., is located in the Sheboygan Industrial Park at 3322 Washington Avenue.

standards, but also must meet all industry and governmental requirements, including the Underwriters' Laboratories label.

The firm's goal is to produce a unique identity for its clients through the use of a Kieffer sign, whether it be through the faithful reproduction of the client's present logo or a totally new logo developed by Kieffer's expert designers.

With Steve Kieffer as president and his brother, Tom, as vice-president, Kieffer & Co., Inc., will continue to grow and prosper—because with Kieffer, the sky is the limit.

ST. NICHOLAS HOSPITAL

Four members of the Hospital Sisters of the Third Order of St. Francis arrived in Sheboygan in 1890. Their mission was to provide care for the sick and poor in the community. Ever since then St. Nicholas Hospital and its sponsors, the Hospital Sisters, have maintained a proud tradition of meeting the health care needs of the area's residents.

a $17-million facility, built on the west side of the city, which the staff moved into in 1979.

The community has been an equal partner in the hospital's plans to care for area residents through modern facilities and equipment. Beginning with donations of $824, given to the Sisters one year after their arrival, the community has been an ardent

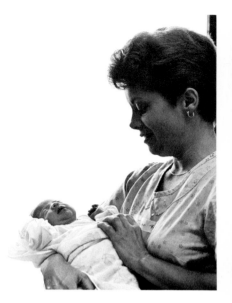

Mothers and babies have a close relationship from the start in the Genesis Center, where three birthing rooms allow patients to labor, deliver, and recover in the same room.

The Hospital Sisters established St. Nicholas Hospital in 1890 and have maintained its proud tradition of meeting the health care needs of Sheboygan residents.

Those four Sisters would not recognize today's health care delivery system. However, they would recognize the same philosophy guiding the actions of the current hospital administration and staff. The Hospital Sisters' mission of providing kind, compassionate health care and ensuring the highest professional and ethical standards of medical competence and leadership has been consistent through the years.

Several building programs have been instrumental in allowing St. Nicholas Hospital to dispense care in a timely and cost-efficient manner. The most recent construction project culminated in

supporter of the institution.

Technological advancements in the health care field occur on an ongoing basis. These improvements have increased the accuracy of diagnosis and changed the methods of providing treatment. The hospital keeps abreast of these advancements and utilizes the latest and most appropriate equipment available.

A state-of-the-art linear accelerator has been installed in the hospital's newly constructed radiation

therapy department. This department is an integral part of the hospital's Community Cancer Care Center. The center, which incorporates an oncology unit, outpatient chemotherapy and transfusion treatment area, and two family room suites, offers a coordinated approach to the diagnosis, treatment, care, and support of cancer patients and their families.

The installation of an in-house CT scan unit has improved the diagnostic capability for persons needing tests on this sophisticated equipment. It has also increased the comfort and convenience level for both inpatients and outpatients.

The risks associated with exposure to anesthesia during surgery have been significantly reduced by the use of SARA (System for Anesthesia and Respiratory Analysis). This equipment ensures that the safest-possible and lowest level of anesthetic drugs is used during surgery. Its use in the operating, recovery, and intensive care rooms allows the anesthesia staff to monitor the exact level of blood gases at any time during the surgery and recovery period.

St. Nicholas Hospital's maternity unit, the Genesis Center, offers a safe, comfortable birthing experience for women and their families. Three large, pleasantly decorated birthing rooms allow patients to labor, deliver, and recover in the same room.

Persons needing hemodialysis have convenient access to St. Nicholas Hospital's renal dialysis unit. The unit features six stations, along with Continuous Ambulatory Peritoneal Dialysis (CAPD) training and support. CAPD patients have the freedom to receive dialysis without being attached to a permanent machine, allowing them to continue near-normal daily routines.

Modern equipment is found in nearly every department of the hospital. This equipment includes a YAG-laser for ophthalmological surgery, a dedicated low-dose mammography unit, and rare earth imaging equipment to provide X-rays that give the lowest-possible exposure to radiation.

Emergency medical care is administered by the highly skilled emergency team 24 hours a day. The hospital's emergency department holds an intermediate classification in emergency services. The institution is served by the Flight for Life helicopter service.

In response to a community need for services to aid battered adults, the hospital has operated the Domestic Violence Prevention Center since 1978. Shelter and counseling services are available, without charge, to any person suffering from physical or emotional violence.

St. Nicholas Hospital is committed to caring not only for the sick, but also to helping people prevent illness and disease. The

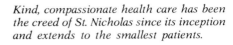

Kind, compassionate health care has been the creed of St. Nicholas since its inception and extends to the smallest patients.

health promotion department is focused on making individuals aware of their state of health, and helping them to achieve optimal health. Classes and workshops on appropriate life-style changes and self-examination techniques are offered on a regular basis to the public. This health promotion effort extends to local work places, with

St. Nicholas Hospital keeps abreast of the latest diagnostic equipment such as this CT scan unit.

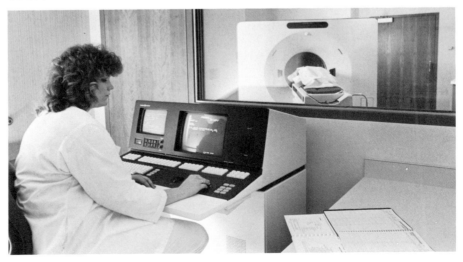

special programs that introduce wellness to employees.

A mobile health sevice van, the first of its kind in the state, takes health information to the people. The Health Express travels to outlying communities and makes visits to special events in the community to offer health screenings and information to the general public.

The original Sisters who brought health care to Sheboygan often provided their services in patients' homes. An extension of this first outreach program continues today. Respiratory therapy, rehabilitation therapy, dietary assistance, and social services are now provided outside the hospital to those needing continuing care or short-term assistance in regaining a normal life-style following illness or surgery.

While keeping its action in step with the mission of its founders, St. Nicholas Hospital continues to evaluate new technology and treatment modalities in order to give its patients quality, professional care, delivered with kindness and

S&R CHEESE CORPORATION

Paul Sartori, who had humble beginnings in northern Italy, migrated to this country in 1907. With no knowledge of the English language he began by helping to build the Pennsylvania Station in New York, 100 feet below the surface, working 10 hours a day in two feet of water for 12.5 cents an hour. He worked at times as a sandhog in the subway under the East River, as a steel mine employee in a Canadian mine, and in the grocery business in upper Minnesota. In the small town of Buhl, Minnesota, he became chief of police and then postmaster for 14 years. Finding that type of work too soft, he left Minnesota to join the Stella Cheese Company in Chicago, where he served as sales manager for 10 years.

While working at the cheese company Sartori became acquainted with Louis Rossini, another employee who later helped found the S&R Cheese Company in Plymouth, Wisconsin.

Sartori had not forgotten the little town in Italy. The town conferred upon him in 1955 the honorary title of Knight of Merit of the Italian Republic. This title was bestowed upon Sartori for his generosity in aiding destitute families in his native village. Sartori later conceived the idea of a home for the poor and the aged, and donated all of the money for its construction and perpetual care. In his memoirs he explained that during the Depression his father sent him money from Italy, and he felt it was time to return it to the people in Italy.

Rossini, who had been in charge of production for the Stella Cheese Company and thus had a long history in the Italian cheese industry, brought to S&R Cheese Company the practical working knowledge of the day-to-day man-

Farmers deliver milk to the original cheese factory in 1910. This building was occupied by S&R Cheese Corporation in 1939 and is still in use today.

ufacture of Italian cheese. Joining Sartori and Rossini was a third partner, Joseph Sartori, Paul's son. Joseph was a graduate of the University of Wisconsin, completing the course in dairy technology in the College of Agriculture in 1938. The original welcoming article in the *Plymouth Review* on May 10, 1939, states, "Young Sartori, while comparatively young, is much enthused over the future of the newly formed enterprise, and anxious to give his technical knowledge toward its success."

When S&R first began to make Italian cheese in May 1939, milk for manufacturing generally cost one dollar per hundredweight, and provolone cheese was selling for approximately 14 cents per pound.

This thriving enterprise actually began on a mere $15,000 capital structure. Its slow, solid growth, spanning almost 50 years to its top rating in the Italian cheese industry, has reflected the pride and application of three generations of the Sartori family.

Arthur Zelm, managing partner with Walter Grasse in the Plymouth Dairy Products Com-

pany, offered to sell cheese milk from his own supply to the new S&R Cheese Company to whatever extent it needed to get started. In the first week or so that amount was a cautious 5,000 pounds of milk per day. The first batch, 500 pounds of provolone cheese made on May 10, 1939, has today burgeoned to an annual production of some 30 million pounds, distributed throughout the United States and abroad. This output includes provolone, mozzarella, Romano, Parmesan, and grated cheese.

In 1943 the S&R Cheese Company took over the original Plymouth Dairy Products manufacturing facility, and that same year bought the old Plymouth Brewing Company site (across the street) for its office and storage facilities.

World War II and its strictures exerted strong influences on the cheese business, making supplies of necessary materials difficult to obtain and requiring innovative research on the part of S&R to remain viable. One of the firm's most important pioneering efforts was the search for a satisfactory replacement for rennet paste. Originally made in Italy, it was then still used for both clotting and flavor development. S&R led the way in promoting the use of a new purified flavoring enzyme developed by the Dairyland Food Laboratories of Waukesha, Wisconsin. This enzyme in modern form is today in common use by the entire Italian cheese industry.

In 1943 S&R shared in the establishment of American Producers of Italian Type Cheese Association (APITCA) in Fond du Lac. Later Paul Sartori, and then Joseph Sartori, headed this important national organization.

The firm was also the first to try to promote the now commonly adopted use of Cryovac for the vacuum packing of Italian cheeses—over opposition by others in the industry.

In the early 1940s Paul Sartori was granted two U.S. patents for curd mixing and kneading machines, which led to the present common use of more sophisticated equipment.

In 1953 Joseph Sartori and Leonard Gentine, Sr., founded the Sargento Cheese Company in order to expand the market for Italian cheese by offering consumer-size packages to the growing retail trade. Previously there had been no access to that form of Italian or many other types of cheese. Tremendous leaps have been made since then in both retail and bulk demand for Italian cheese throughout the country. In 1968 the Gentine family took over the Sartori interests in Sargento, which remains first nationally in this specialized field.

In early 1955 the Rossini family relinquished its interest in the firm. At that time, and until recent years, a daughter of Paul Sartori, Ada Catchpole, as well as the nine children of Joseph Sartori, still retained original shares in the company. After Paul Sartori's death in 1957, Joe Sartori took over the reins and brought into active management his three sons, Dante Camilli as vice-president, and Guido Sartori, a cousin, as secretary/treasurer.

Today's officers include James Sartori, president; Paul Sartori, vice-president/procurement; Steve Sartori, secretary/treasurer; Dante Camilli, vice-president/production; and Shannon Barrett, chief financial officer. Joseph Sartori became board chairman in 1987 after 31 years as president of the firm. The corporation has recently purchased the complete interest of Joseph's sister, Ada, and that of his six daughters, making the S&R Cheese Corporation fully owned by Joseph Sartori's three sons.

Joseph Sartori is confident that the continued growth and impact of the firm, on both a local and a national level, will proceed even more vigorously under the direction he set for them, and with the efforts of the third generation of the Sartori family.

Joseph Sartori (second from left), chairman of the board and son of one of the founders of S&R Cheese Corporation, with sons (from left) James, president; Paul, vice-president/procurement; and Steve, secretary/treasurer, examining provolone cheese in the curing room.

SHEBOYGAN MEMORIAL MEDICAL CENTER

On a chilly January day in 1933, nearly 20,000 Sheboygan area residents waited in a block-long line outside of Sheboygan Memorial Hospital to tour the new 94-bed facility.

The name itself, Sheboygan Memorial Hospital, paid tribute not only to the late Eliza Prange, who willed more than $200,000 in 1928 to the dream of a new hospital, but also to the spirit of Sheboygan residents who saw the dream fulfilled. It was primarily Sheboygan's Lutheran community that showed good faith in meeting the first conditions of Miss Prange's will by depositing an additional $100,000 in Security National Bank for the hospital's building fund.

Skepticism was echoed by some in the community who believed it would be impossible to raise the additional funds necessary to build the hospital during the hard economic times of the 1920s. Others felt, however, that

Though times were hard, ground was broken for Sheboygan Memorial Hospital on July 10, 1931.

public interest in financing a new hospital might be stifled if it was delayed. In 1930 an army of 300 volunteers contacted 5,000 homes, as well as organizations and businesses, in an intense one-week period to overwhelmingly exceed their goal of $250,000 by raising an additional sum of $72,865.

By July 10, 1931, a groundbreaking ceremony laid the cornerstone for the new Sheboygan Memorial Hospital. Hundreds of residents watched as Prange's will, accounts of the hospital fundraising campaign, the histories of the hospital association and Sheboygan, speeches, coins, newspaper articles, and lists of participants' names were placed in the box. Inscribed in the cornerstone was the message: "That human hands might build a structure to alleviate pain and suffering."

It took a year and a half to complete the five-story, labor of love hospital building in 1933. And it took Memorial's first superintendent, R.N. Esther Klingmann, many hours that extended far into the night to personally greet each visitor who came to that dedica-

Through the generosity of Eliza Prange and her bequest of more than $200,000, the dream of a new Sheboygan hospital became a reality.

tion.

In 1950 the first Expectant Mothers' Clinic, an instructional and social event, was planned at Sheboygan Memorial Hospital. The percentage of home births was still significant, but mortality rates and technology made deliver-

ing a baby in the hospital increasingly acceptable as a safer way to deliver.

Approximately two decades ago, mothers and fathers began to shape the future of maternity care at Sheboygan Memorial Hospital. Today ultrasound images produced without radiation enhance diagnosis in obstetrics. Expectant mothers find the hospital atmosphere geared to their comfort. The mothers and their families also receive the emotional and skilled support necessary to make their birthing experience as satisfying as possible.

The first total knee joint implant in Sheboygan, by a team of orthopedic surgeons at Memorial in 1973, began a new chapter in the use of artificial joints. Artificial implants, heralded in the early 1970s, are now routinely performed on shoulders, ankles, elbows, wrists, hips, and knees. Changes in equipment, anesthesia, and specialization have all made their mark on modern surgical capabilities. But the biggest breakthrough at Memorial today may be the increased availability of outpatient surgery. Same-day surgery in Memorial's Surgi-Center is now used for procedures that once required lengthy hospitalizations.

With medical specialization and continued research, each day brings new hope for patients and providers of health care at Memorial. Skilled emergency care and efficient transport service assures patients of receiving prompt quality care. Memorial's intensive and coronary care unit provides patients with around-the-clock nursing with the most modern heart-monitoring and life-support systems available. Sophisticated diagnostic services from laboratory to radiology can help detect diseases and seek out potential problems.

Unlike the hospital wards of yesteryear, all Memorial patients receive care in private rooms equipped with telephones, televisions, private baths, colorful draperies, carpeting, and wooden cabinets.

Although every aspect of today's hospital care is touched by changing technology, diagnostic services in particular have felt the greatest impact of new machines in their work. The addition of the mobile CT (computerized tomography) scanner to the array of radiology services offered adds a new dimension to patient diagnosis. The scanner blends X ray and a computer to provide detailed images of a cross section of body tissue for in-depth analysis. The image created can be likened to examining a single slice of bread without cutting into the loaf.

More is the key word in comparing modern Sheboygan Memorial Medical Center with hospitals of 50 years ago. Today there is more individual nursing care, more medical specialization, and more emphasis on training and education. Consumer demand for quality health care, increased services, more patient comforts, and fewer hospital beds have all helped shape contemporary general hospitals.

Today the medical center is a major Sheboygan institution, employing close to 650 workers, with a payroll approaching $9 million. Expanding services, new technology, and sophisticated staff training have helped Sheboygan Memorial preserve and improve on the

Today the hospital is equipped with all of the latest amenities, including birthing rooms where the warmth and homelike atmosphere make it a much less frightening experience.

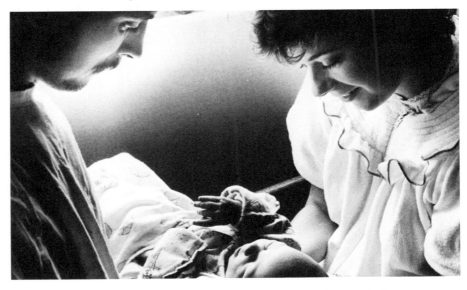

quality of life in Sheboygan.

"The list of modern 'miracle' services is endless," says Patrick Trotter, president of Sheboygan Memorial Medical Center. "But the key to providing quality medical care is keeping our staff well versed in newly recognized syndromes, as well as trained in new treatment and techniques. Only by keeping up with the demands of changing medical technology and specialized medicine have we been able to continue offering our patients quality service and life-saving care."

FIRST WISCONSIN SOUTH WEST BANK

South-West State Bank of Sheboygan was organized in 1923 with Oscar Zimbal as president. The institution not only filled a community need for a high-grade banking service in the southwest section of the city, but also provided a convenience to farmers for their banking needs.

When Oscar Zimbal died in 1926, Roland J. Herr became president of South-West State Bank. Under Herr's conservative management, the institution's business grew to such an extent that a new building was constructed on South 12th Street.

Over the years the 2.5-block stretch on the south side of Sheboygan became a thriving business community that was nicknamed Little Sheboygan. With this growth, South-West State Bank also flourished, requiring it to build a larger structure in 1974, a few doors north of its original location. The new building, a one-story structure costing more than $600,000, featured the latest in bank design and equipment.

According to president Robert A. Meissner, who succeeded Joseph F. Bauman and directed the institution for 11 years, South-West State Bank's consistent growth and prosperity enabled it to become the third-largest banking institution in Sheboygan County.

In 1985 South-West State Bank merged with the First Wisconsin Corporation and changed its name to First Wisconsin South West Bank of Sheboygan.

A year later James M. Bichler, president of South West, headed the newly formed Heritage Square Merchants Association. Its membership represents 21 businesses and professional services on South 12th Street. Its objective is to revitalize the four-square-block section of the city's south side and to encourage the business owners on South 12th Street to renovate and restore their existing property. First Wisconsin South West Bank has allocated $500,000 in low-interest loans to finance building acquisitions and improvements.

With the bank's role as a catalyst in lending money for redevelopment, the association's goals of filling vacant buildings, remodeling existing structures while preserving the historical architecture, expanding parking, and pursuing a housing project for the elderly seem attainable.

Many merchants in the area believe potential investors may be attracted to the business and professional opportunities available on Heritage Square. "We're a neighborhood bank," Bichler says, "and we're committed to our neighbors. Any success they enjoy will further the success of our bank."

From an institution that started 65 years ago with two employees and original deposits of $63,000, to its present work force of 40 people and deposits of $61 million, First Wisconsin South West Bank continues to be the third-largest bank in Sheboygan County and one of Sheboygan's friendliest.

The South-West State Bank of Sheboygan (left) was located in the 12th Street business district (below) in the 1930s.

The First Wisconsin South West Bank of today.

JOS. SCHMITT & SONS CONSTRUCTION COMPANY, INC.

Jos. Schmitt & Sons Construction Company, Inc., is a family operation steeped in a tradition of excellence in contracting and construction. The firm has grown and prospered as a result of individual and mutual commitment to that family tradition.

Joseph Schmitt started his construction business in 1899 after having served his carpenter apprenticeship with the railroad. Working on his own, Schmitt started constructing private residences, farms, and church buildings in and around the Sheboygan area where he earned a reputation for fair dealing and fine craftsmanship.

Joseph's son, Robert, joined the business in 1931, and the company was incorporated as Jos. Schmitt & Son, Inc. Also at that time, in addition to building, the firm engaged in general contracting and real estate.

In 1945 Robert M. Schmitt bought the company from his father and was joined by his two sons, Donald and Richard. The corporate name was then changed to Jos. Schmitt & Sons Construction Company, Inc., with business consisting of designing and remodeling homes as well as commercial buildings.

Donald R. Schmitt bought the business from his father in 1961. Seven years later, due to the firm's rapid growth, new offices and mill work facilities were constructed at 2104 Union Avenue. In 1977 the office space was expanded and a warehouse added. In addition, Jos. Schmitt & Sons Construction Company acquired

metal building and overhead door franchises to better serve its commercial and industrial clients. As a result of its commitment to excellence, Jos. Schmitt & Sons has received numerous awards for its innovative plan interpretations, superior construction, and quality workmanship.

On July 22, 1986, a year before the overhead door business was moved to 2602 Georgia Avenue, Donald Schmitt died. His son, Steven J. Schmitt, had become president at the time of his father's retirement a year earlier.

Today the fourth generation of the Schmitt family—Reed J. Schmitt, treasurer, and Loretta E. Schmitt (wife of Donald), secretary—is providing professional contracting, construction, and real estate services to a community where its roots have been embedded for more than 80 years. From those traditional commitments by the family-owned company and the many fine businesses and residents in the Sheboygan County area, the

Donald R. Schmitt, president from 1961 to 1985.

Schmitt family gratefully looks forward to continuing to serve the community's needs.

With its reputation for excellence built upon a strong foundation of past successes, Jos. Schmitt & Sons Construction Company, Inc., is uniquely qualified and well prepared to meet the present and future needs of its clients.

Officers of the family-owned and -operated construction company include (from left) Roy E. Ten Pas, vice-president; Loretta E. Schmitt, secretary; Steven J. Schmitt, president; and Reed J. Schmitt, treasurer.

K.W. MUTH COMPANY
MUTH WOOD-STOCK COMPANY/
AMERICAN WOOD-STOCK COMPANY

New American Wood-Stock Company facility built in 1987 in the Sheboygan Industrial Park.

K.W. Muth Company was founded by Kenneth W. Muth in a one-car garage in Sheboygan in 1946. The main revenue of the business in its early years came from the sale of paper-packaging items.

At its present location on Muth Court the firm now encompasses 240,000 square feet and has approximately 600 employees. Its main focus is the North American automobile market, producing insulated components, acoustical and thermal, for floor, door, roof, engine compartment, and cargo areas of cars and trucks. In addition, through its newest technology, Wood-Stock, it provides interior soft-trim components such as door panels, bucket seat backs, and trunk/cargo area sheet-metal covers. These trim parts are covered in carpet, vinyl, or cloth and then laminated, molded, and cut in the one-step patented Wood-Stock process. The Wood-Stock material is a moldable sheet produced by extruding a blend of wood flour and various plastic resins.

In 1984 two new companies were founded based upon the Italian-developed Wood-Stock technology. The K.W. Muth people and their Italian partners formed the American Wood-Stock Company to produce the moldable sheet stock. It operates in its new facilities in the Sheboygan Industrial Park. The Muth Wood-Stock Company, which is located in the recently expanded K.W. Muth Company plant, transforms the Wood-Stock material into various trim components.

The three organizations operate as related entities and share the same marketing, managerial, operational, and personnel policies. Collectively their strategy is to be profitable by providing world-class goods and services as measured by their quality, dependability, and technology; they are dedicated in using materials that are friendly to the environment, recyclable, and preferably reclaimable; they recognize the need to operate as a global organization; and they recognize their obligation to their employees and Sheboygan County.

As a matter of philosophy employees share in annual profits and all pertinent information. Further, all three companies support local agencies and nonprofit organizations, and strive to raise the standard of living in Sheboygan County.

Looking to the future, K.W. Muth Company, Muth Wood-Stock Company, and American Wood-Stock Company are growth oriented. Sheboygan County has been the home of each of the three organizations since their inception. While it is planned that satellite operations in other locations may be necessary to protect the competitive position of the combined organization in the future, Sheboygan is the home office and base of all operations and has proven to be an ideal location.

K.W. Muth Company, Muth Wood-Stock Company, and American Wood-Stock Company are committed to Sheboygan.

These were the K.W. Muth Company facilities in 1959.

VINYL PLASTICS, INC.

Shortly after the end of World War II a group of Sheboygan investors decided to form a company called Natural Products, Inc. Their purpose was to utilize some of the technology developed during the war years in the manufacture and use of a new type of plastic: polyvinyl chloride (PVC).

The firm's first manufacturing facility was set up in an old factory building on 18th Street and Erie Avenue. After two years of struggling with used equipment and a team of East Coast technical experts, the fledgling organization, under the leadership of Ben W. Harff, began to focus its attention on the manufacture of vinyl floor tile. This effort, too, got off to a shaky start as employees struggled to master the new technology and to establish a level of quality with which the company could be proud.

In 1950 Natural Products, Inc., was reorganized as Vinyl Plastics, Inc. (VPI); a year later Robert E. Kohler joined the firm as president. It was also in the early 1950s that VPI introduced Conductile, the first vinyl flooring specially de-

signed to dissipate static electricity. During the late 1950s and 1960s VPI broadened market recognition and acceptance of its other tile products, opening sales on a worldwide basis.

With its product growth and its increased work force, VPI's Erie Avenue plant became inadequate. In 1968 the firm relocated to South Ninth Street, adding offices to an existing manufacturing and warehouse building.

For VPI the 1970s were a tumultuous decade filled with change. The company struggled with declining sales as a result of interruptions of production stemming from the plant relocation, minimal profits, oil shortages that limited availability of raw materials, and the general economy in the United States slowing commercial construction, therefore, decreasing the market for flooring.

During that period a decision was made to enter the vinyl sheeting and film business with the introduction of high-quality packaging materials. Sheeting manufacturing was first introduced in the Sheboygan plant; that process

Vinyl Plastics, Inc., has grown into an international competitor operating out of this headquarters facility on Ninth Street in Sheboygan and additional facilities in Sheboygan Falls and Manitowoc.

became successful and, as a result, the firm outgrew its facilities. The company then purchased an additional facility in Sheboygan Falls in 1975; 12 years later it acquired another facility in Montville, New Jersey.

In the early 1980s, in order to further diversify its product line, VPI began to experiment with the use of reclaimed vinyl in the production of filled-vinyl products in slab and sheet form. The success of this effort led to the acquisition of a third facility in Manitowoc.

Today Vinyl Plastics, Inc., employs more than 225 people and successfully competes on a worldwide basis. Quality is the company's number-one operating priority, reflected in its philosophy: Concentrate on prevention rather than inspection to make quality a way of life, and perpetuate an attitude of "Do it right the first time."

SCHREIER MALTING COMPANY

Like many Sheboygan-based businesses, the Schreier Malting Company was born of the entrepreneurial inclinations of an immigrant. In 1843 Theodore Schreier departed Guntersblum on the Rhein in a Germany torn by reformation and political upheavals to bring his family—including 13-year-old Konrad Schreier—to Washington County, Wisconsin.

Konrad grew up on his family's farm a few miles northwest of Milwaukee. In 1851 he obtained his own farm, which he sold five years later to move to Sheboygan where he established a brewery and malthouse in partnership with H. Schlicht. Six years later Konrad bought out his partner and conducted the business under his own name until 1896, when it was incorporated as the Konrad Schreier Company.

Konrad and Elizabeth Schreier had three children: Mary Elizabeth (who married Louis A. Testwuide), Herman, and Emma (who married Alfred P. Steffen). Konrad served as company president until 1896, when he was succeeded by Herman Schreier.

In 1911 one of the largest fires in Sheboygan history destroyed the wooden elevator and malthouse at the Konrad Schreier Company. They were replaced by a concrete elevator and malthouse, which had a storage capacity of 500,000 bushels and a malting capacity of one million bushels. At the time the brewery's annual capacity was 50,000 barrels, indicating that malting had become the firm's primary business.

Like most brewers, the Konrad Schreier Company had its own network of taverns. In the years immediately before the Volstead Act became the law of the land, Schreier owned 28 taverns in Sheboygan. Its only compet-

itor had 18. This was during a period when the Schlitz brewery was reputed to be one of the largest holders of urban real estate in the United States.

During Prohibition the Schreier brewery and malthouse shut down, but the firm stayed afloat with a small soft drink business conducted out of the bottle house. Schreier bottled such brand names as Green River, Cherry Blossom, Orange Crush, Dublin Dry Ginger Ale, and Coca-Cola.

In the mid-1920s the Coca-Cola Bottling Company wanted Schreier to drop its other soft drink brands and become the exclusive Coke franchisee for a large portion of Wisconsin. Deciding it would be impossible to operate with only one brand of soda, Schreier management rejected the offer. As a company official later observed, "History had recorded that this was a big mistake—but anyone can second guess!"

In spite of the soft drink business and a try at going into the whole wheat flour business, the firm lost money every year during the period from 1920 to 1930. To keep going, Schreier gradually sold off the nonmalting properties it had accumulated over the years, including the taverns and the brewery. The 1930 sale of the brewery, which was destined to permanently close in a few years, provided Schreier with enough of a cash flow to renovate its malthouse and to serve the United States brewing industry, which was anxiously awaiting the repeal of the 18th Amendment.

The repeal did not come soon enough, however, to save hundreds of brewers and brewing industry suppliers, and Schreier's survival of that bizarre period was

Fifth-generation family member Thomas R. Testwuide is the current president and chief executive officer of Schreier Malting Company.

no certainty as the following quote from a corporate history indicates: "If repeal had not occurred as soon as it did, the Konrad Schreier Company may have gone out of business."

By April 7, 1933, the legalization of beer renewed the demand for malt, and the Konrad Schreier Company soon began to regain its strength. Small additions to malting capacity were made in 1933, 1936, and 1950; storage capacity was expanded in 1933, 1936, and 1939. The corporation assumed its present name, the Schreier Malting Company, in 1935.

During the 1940s and 1950s the firm served many local and regional breweries and enjoyed fairly stable operations. But the trend that was to alter the structure of the U.S. brewing industry and pose new challenges for its suppliers was already evident.

The well-chronicled thinning of the ranks that pared the roster of operating breweries from 770 just after the repeal, to 200 by

The Schreier Malting Company facility in Sheboygan.

1963, and to fewer than 50 by 1979 was accompanied by a realignment in the malting industry. The surviving malting companies were those willing and able to adapt to the changes that drastically transformed the structure of their primary client industry.

In the early 1970s the leaders of the Schreier Malting Company elected to meet the challenges posed by this transformation. Also, it was clear that to remain viable in the malting industry, Schreier would have to go into the barley procurement business.

Happily for all concerned, Thomas R. Testwuide, son of Robert L. Testwuide, and his strategists opted for growth rather than liquidation. By the end of 1987 the firm had an annual production capacity of 8 million bushels. It has served, among others, nine of the nation's largest brewers, and is vertically integrated with grain procurement capability, storage capacity, and quality control and research facilities to effectively face the challenge of the future.

Thomas R. Testwuide, chief executive officer, is a fifth-generation descendant of Konrad Schreier. The succession of Schreier presidents following Herman was Alfred P. Steffen, 1926-1930; Konrad Testwuide (son of Louis), 1930-1957; and Robert L. Testwuide (son of Konrad), 1957-1973.

Schreier Malting Company's corporate charter states: "Schreier is a quality processor of malt and grain, operated by motivated professionals, tailoring consistent products, clean, efficient operations, and timely deliveries to profitably meet the present and growing needs of its customers."

Thomas Testwuide is pleased with the growth and success of Schreier Malting Company and is convinced that the firm will soon be at another crossroads. "We have to be prepared to grow larger as greater demand comes for our product, which is widely recognized in the brewing industry for its excellent quality."

H.C. PRANGE COMPANY

The year 1987 marks the 100th anniversary of the H.C. Prange Company. It is now one of the largest family-owned department store chains in the country.

Its origins began with a poor Sheboygan Falls farm boy who was sickly. When Henry C. Prange's father died in 1876, leaving a large family behind on a small farm, Prange became the sole wage earner. Not being physically strong enough to do farm work, Prange secured employment in a grocery/general store as a clerk, janitor, and delivery boy. Eleven years later Prange, along with his sister, Eliza, and a brother-in-law, J.H. Bitter, opened their own general/grocery store in the city of Sheboygan in a 3,300-square-foot building and called it H.C. Prange.

The store became such a rapid success that in 1898 it was incorporated as the H.C. Prange Company. By 1923 a new store was built on the same site, with more than 180,000 square feet making it the largest store in Wisconsin out-

Sheboygan's H.C. Prange Company celebrated its 100th anniversary in 1987. Photo circa 1909

side of Milwaukee.

Before Prange's death in 1928 the H.C. Prange Company had become a multimillion-dollar business with hundreds of employees that were referred to as "associates." Upon his father's death H. Carl Prange, while in his mid-twenties, was given the responsibility of running the company.

H. Carl Prange's goal in 1930, during the stock market crash, was to do one million dollars in the grocery business, and $2 million in dry goods. During the Depression, while still heavily in debt from the 1927 purchase of the Hall Dry Goods building in Green Bay, Prange acquired the L.M. Washburn Company of Sturgeon Bay and opened the firm's third

store. In 1935 a disastrous fire burned the Sturgeon Bay store to the ground. A short five months after the fire, a new store was built. The year 1946 saw the purchase of Appleton's Pettibone-Peabody store, one of the oldest retail organizations in the state.

Over the years more acquisitions were made by the H.C. Prange Company, and existing stores underwent continuous improvements to keep abreast of the times. Today the H.C. Prange Company operates 21 department stores, 20 Prange Way stores, and 106 id stores. In addition, the firm operates a Business Interiors facility in Green Bay and two Christmas & Things shops in Florida.

Fifty years ago there was a family-owned department store in almost every community in the country. Today you can almost count the remaining stores on one hand. The H.C. Prange Company's belief in value, fashion, and satisfaction affirm its customer service policy: "It's Not Yours 'Til You Like It!" Now the century-old organization has more than 10,000 employees and only three chief executive officers from three generations of the founding family running the business.

Service has been an H.C. Prange Company hallmark from the beginning. "It's Not Yours 'Til You Like It" continues to be the company commitment. Photo circa 1915

WIGWAM MILLS, INC.

A year after the Sheboygan Knitting Company, founded by Lawrence Bentz, burned down in 1904, the Hand Knit Hosiery Company was created. The first products manufactured by the Hand Knit Hosiery Company, of which Herbert Chesebro was president, were heavy woolen socks and liner mittens for the lumbermen.

Four years later the hosiery firm constructed a new building at the corner of 14th Street and Huron Avenue. This facility became the headquarters for all the company's operations. At some point between 1914 and 1917 a second building was constructed to be used as a warehouse and office, leaving the original building for manufacturing.

By 1922 Herbert Chesebro gained partial control of the Hand Knit Hosiery Company by buying Lawrence Bentz' shares. Under Chesebro's presidency the company grew and flourished.

When the stock market crashed and the Great Depression began, the Hand Knit Hosiery Company fell upon hard times. With the economy taking its toll on the hosiery business, the Hand Knit Hosiery Company, after Chesebro's death, struggled under the burden of bank loans totaling $100,000. With the help of J.W. Hansen of the Citizen's Bank, the company stayed in business.

In 1936 Robert E. Chesebro, Herbert's son, after having worked at the firm for 12 years, gained complete control of the Hand Knit Hosiery Company.

In 1941, when the Japanese bombed Pearl Harbor, the Hand Knit Hosiery Company also went to war—75 percent of its production was devoted to providing heavy wool socks for the Army. To keep pace with a growing product and greater sales, a third building was added that year at the same site. A year later an addition was made to the dyehouse, and a new boiler was added. By 1945 production included baseball hosiery, anklets, hockey caps, mittens and linear mittens, and athletic, hunting, bundle, boot, skating, and bed socks.

On January 1, 1957, a major event was marked by changing the name of the company to Wigwam Mills, Inc.

In 1969 Wigwam Mills purchased 16 acres of land on Crocker Avenue in the Sheboygan Industrial Park, and within a year constructed a new 38,000-square-

Wigwam Mills, Inc., is headquartered in this facility on Crocker Avenue in the Sheboygan Industrial Park. Originally known as the Hand Knit Hosiery Company, the firm has been a major Sheboygan employer since 1905.

foot building housing a completely modern dyehouse and a boarding and finishing department. The main plant continued at the original location. Then, in 1974, the entire operation, including the main plant on Huron Avenue, was moved to the Sheboygan Industrial Park in a new 200,000-square-foot facility that incorporated the 38,000-square-foot structure.

Today Wigwam Mills, Inc., is a thriving business with a work force of nearly 400; the strength and success of the company is attributed to dedicated employees, quality products, good customers, and a dedicated sports and fitness-conscious public.

With Robert E. Chesebro, Jr., the third generation of Chesebros running the company, Wigwam Mills, Inc., has gained the reputation for not only supplying a quality product, but also for its service, innovation in product development, and integrity.

LAKE TO LAKE DAIRY

The Lake to Lake Sheboygan fluid milk plant got its start in 1902, when a group of farmers banded together and formed the Sheboygan Dairymen's Association. The organization continued as such until 1929, when the group incorporated as the Sheboygan Dairymen's Cooperative Association. A year later the group started in business as the Modern Dairy Cooperative by purchasing a building at 2715 North 15th Street.

In the spring of 1930 another plant was opened on the northeast corner of Erie Avenue and 16th Street for the purpose of retailing fluid milk and other dairy products. The undertaking proved so successful that the business developed to the point where 20 milk routes were needed to distribute the bottled milk and dairy products to other retail trade of the Modern Dairy Cooperative. This distribution was done by horse-drawn wagons equipped with pneumatic tires and horses shod

An outdoor conveyor belt helps with the loading of trucks for home delivery in 1958.

Milk being packaged in the 1980s in plastic, one-gallon containers that were manufactured at the Sheboygan plant, which is now closed.

with rubber shoes.

The retail business took approximately one-quarter of the milk supplied by the members, while the balance was being converted into powdered whole milk, bulk condensed milk, butter, and American cheese. Practically all of the butter manufactured, and a substantial share of the American cheese, went directly to the retail trade of the Modern Dairy Cooperative.

By 1942 the organization's membership consisted of 200 farmers, with 50 people working in the plant. At that time Modern Dairy was also serving nearly 5,000 families in Kohler, Sheboygan, and Sheboygan Falls on its retail routes. Its daily production of cheese was approximately 2,500 pounds, or 1.25 tons per day, which required 25,000 to 30,000 pounds of milk, all of which was sold to local concerns and shipped nationwide.

Modern Dairy, after losing some of its markets and having a surplus of milk, decided to merge with Lake to Lake in 1956. Almost immediately the company began to expand its business to other surrounding areas. Over the years the firm went from glass bottles to paper to plastic packaging for its products, and made acquisitions of dairies in neighboring counties.

During the 1980s the full-line fluid milk plant took up one full block in the city, had 105 employees, and bottled more than 500,000 pounds of milk per week. The Sheboygan facility was also one of the first milk plants in the area to implement foil seals on plastic milk containers, and the first to bring the computer into the processing operation. In 1987 Lake to Lake consolidated its bottling operation with Golden Guernsey, Waukesha.

Quality standards are a key element in the success of the Lake to Lake Dairy plant, along with the quality milk supplied by the cooperative's member-owners.

THOMAS INDUSTRIES, INC.

The Electric Sprayit Company moved from Milwaukee's Moe-Bridges factory to Sheboygan in 1939, where it leased an old 1918 vintage factory building that the city had taken over for back taxes. Working with 40 employees, the firm produced compressors, spray guns, and Moe-Bridges lighting fixtures. During World War II Sprayit's work force rose to nearly 700, working three shifts and producing tank turrets and antennae, bomb fuses, fuel pumps for aircraft, and in-air refueling receptacles for B-25 bombers.

In 1953 Thomas Industries, Inc., purchased Electric Sprayit, and while the firm continued renting its Sheboygan plant from the city for 15 years, Thomas eventually purchased the factory at 15th and Illinois Avenue.

Over the next 10 years Thomas Industries acquired other companies in Wisconsin, Arkansas, Illinois, Tennessee, and Canada. It was also during this time that Thomas Industries received President John F. Kennedy's "E" for Export Excellence Award. This award was in recognition of the firm's achievements in successfully expanding its overseas sales.

Due to the company's growth and success, where it more than doubled its export sales, Thomas Industries, requiring a larger facility, built a 126,000-square-foot modern factory in 1975 on a 25-acre site in the Sheboygan Industrial Park. On May 26, 1976, Thomas Industries became a recipient of the president's "E" Star Award in recognition of having demonstrated superior performance in increasing or promoting exports during a three-year period subsequent to its winning the "E" Award.

As a result of further growth, Thomas' sales in 1978 were up 39

percent from the previous year. Of the $115 million in sales in 1979 by the widely diversified 23-plant Thomas Industries chain, the tool and hardware section, of which Sheboygan's Power Air Division is a major component, accounted for nearly $43 million—a 27-percent gain over 1978. Even in 1980, when other industries were feeling the effects of the recession, Thomas' Power Air Division continued to flourish, producing more than 700 different compressors and related products.

In 1985 Thomas Industries, Inc., formed a joint venture between its Power Air Division in Sheboygan and a West Germany manufacturer, ASF GmbH Company, which produced diaphragm compressors/vacuum pumps and

Thomas Industries, Inc., from its beginning in a 1918 vintage factory (left) to the modern Sheboygan Industrial Park (right) site today.

peristaltic liquid pumps.

Today Thomas employs upwards of 325 Sheboygan workers and 3,000 workers in its 15 divisions and subsidiaries in 10 states, Canada, and West Germany. The firm designs, manufactures, and markets lighting products for the home and work environments, as well as specialty products for commercial, industrial, and consumer markets.

The success of Thomas Industries, Inc., is a result of its excellent Sheboygan work force and its commitment to new products that will serve the expanding needs of world markets.

THE H.C. DENISON COMPANY

The H.C. Denison Company serves more than 3,000 accounts and has 12 employees, which is the largest staff of any investment firm in Sheboygan County. Prior to founding the investment company in 1928, Homer C. Denison worked for Babson's statistical organization.

When Denison returned to Sheboygan in 1924, outside of holding AT&T shares there were not more than 25 people in Sheboygan County who had securities on the New York Stock Exchange. Denison served as president of The H.C. Denison Company with Hal Huibregtse as vice-president until 1974, when Konrad C. Testwuide assumed the position of president and became the controlling stockholder. Testwuide joined the firm in 1964, and Dorothy Metscher, now vice-president, came to Denison from another organization in 1972.

In early 1987 the firm purchased Gottsacker Investment Co., at which time Kenneth Goodman, Gottsacker Investment's principal, and Robert Trautschold joined H.C. Denison's staff. Although The H.C. Denison Company is still small compared to most investment operations, it is one of the oldest investment firms in the

state, and one of the few independent operations remaining in business.

With the Testwuide family's history embedded in the community since the mid-1800s, the company reflects a conservative tradition in its investment philosophies. Testwuide believes it is the firm's responsibility to make available to its customers conservative investment securities to allow customers to earn a fair return on their investment consistent with the safety of their principal.

In past years the organization has had to protect its customers' assets against inflation and has suggested that its customers own a fair amount of common stock of

The company officers in 1964 (from left): Harold Huibregtse, Konrad Testwuide, and Homer C. Denison.

The H.C. Denison Company staff today.

U.S. companies that have proven management, sound financial strength, and products that will remain in demand. Testwuide is of the opinion that the personal service and hands-on investment management a small firm offers far outweighs the benefits of bigness.

"While most of the other Wisconsin investment firms have sold out to banks or large insurance companies," Testwuide observes, "I feel H.C. Denison can better

serve its customers by remaining small and independent—where the customer can still talk to the owner."

James Testwuide, upon joining his father's company some years ago, contributed his expertise by installing an in-house computer system capable of processing the many functions required by the expanding business. The firm's revenues have increased from $300,000 in 1982 to more than one million dollars in 1988. This expansion would not have been possible without the effectiveness of the computer system.

While H.C. Denison emphasizes personal service, the concern is to keep its operations at the highest level of automation and efficiency. The belief is that this combination of goals will offer customers the best quality service available.

Even though the mechanics of The H.C. Denison Company's operation have changed over the 60 years, its investment philosophy has remained constant: "To provide sound investments for the conservative needs of our clients."

WEAVER'S INC.

In 1950, after having worked at the Office Supply and Printing Company for 13 years, Carl Weaver decided to start his own business. With two employees and a 500-square-foot store located at 729 New York Avenue, Weaver applied his office supply knowledge and sales ability acquired from going door to door selling his products in Sheboygan to build Weaver's Inc. into the multimillion-dollar operation it is today.

By 1956 Weaver had purchased the entire stock of office supplies and equipment from the Miller Office Supply Company, hired two more employees, and moved the business to South Eighth Street for additional space. Four years later Weaver's Inc. acquired a business machine company that dealt mainly with typewriters, and opened another office supply store across the street from the South Eighth Street location to sell adding machines, typewriters, and other related machine products.

As business continued to expand, more employees were needed and additional business acquisitions were made, including a soap manufacturing firm bought in 1967 called the Rexine Company. After selling soap products for a few years Weaver's discontinued the manufacturing phase of the soap business and established a distribution program for chemical and paper products. Years later Weaver's dropped the Rexine name, and merged the operation into Weaver's Inc.

Over a 10-year span the growth of the company necessitated building a new, one-story, 24,000-square-foot structure in the Sheboygan Industrial Park at 3513 South 32nd Street, with another 8,000 square feet added in 1977. The firm also acquired an office furniture company in Milwaukee. Perceiving an opportunity, Weaver's hired two design and salespeople from the company and started its own Milwaukee-based interior design business at 241 Farwell Avenue called Weaver's Business Interiors.

With this acquisition, Weaver's Inc. experienced an increase in business when it became involved with major corporations in the southeastern Wisconsin area that presently employs 17 people. As a result of the success of these projects, Weaver's Inc. began doing business on a regional basis.

In 1982 Weaver's purchased the Office Supply and Printing Company, an established Sheboygan firm where Carl Weaver learned the office equipment and supply business prior to opening his own store. When Paul Weaver, Carl's son, became president two years later, Weaver's Inc. went through a management and organizational transition where it expanded marketing areas, added salespeople, became fully automated, and emerged strongly committed to continue supplying a quality product within all four product divisions.

Weaver's Inc., a family-owned office supply business, is not just a company dedicated to its customers and its 55 full-time employees, but also to the community that it services with business supply needs for offices, factories, and homes.

Carl Weaver, founder.

Paul C. Weaver, president.

NEMSCHOFF CHAIRS, INC.

Nemschoff Chairs, Inc., began in 1950, when Leonard M. Nemschoff rented space in the back of a factory building on Virginia Avenue, and, with three employees, started a furniture upholstery job shop. He was soon joined by his brother, Dick, and then his father, Julius. Meeting with immediate success through new ideas and approaches to the market, a year later Nemschoff bought one of the larger manufacturers of upholstered furniture and allied wood products in the Sheboygan County area, and moved the chair company to its present location at 2218 West Water Street.

Innovative ideas were brought forth, and soon Nemschoff was doing business with leading stores and groups in many areas of the country. The firm attracted national recognition from the foremost trade associations, trade press, and all shelter media for outstanding design, consistent quality, integrity, and marketing ideas. In 1962 the company received the American Institute of Designers International Award for seating.

The entire situation in home furnishing merchandising began to change. Former competitors became part of larger companies that, in turn, developed close alliances with the principal retail organizations. Other competitors either retrenched into local area producers on a smaller scale or went out of business. Although Nemschoff could compete product for product, it could not compete with powerful conglomerates and buying group alliances that demanded huge cash outlays for advertising and sales promotions. Soon only marginal small outlets were left as Nemschoff customers.

Nemschoff tried to hold its position, but eventually it became increasingly apparent that the out-

lets to the consumers were diminishing and narrowing with the changes in distribution patterns, and disaster threatened. In 1967 it was determined by the company that Nemschoff Chairs should continue a holding action in home furnishings, while pursuing future growth and expansion in the institutional furnishings field. Two years later Nemschoff Chairs did a complete changeover when its reception in the market reaped excellent results, and the firm found that its reputation for

Nemschoff Chairs, Inc., at 2218 West Water Street and 3115 North 21st Street, has expanded through years of product and sales growth.

quality and service was known to important users.

Management recognition of the geriatric market established a good reputation and relationship with major suppliers in health care, who began to specify Nemschoff products. Although there were many established manufacturers in the institutional field,

for partial refurbishing as well. The success of this planning and effort set the stage for the future growth of the company.

When Joe Miller and Mark Nemschoff joined the firm in the 1970s, they boosted the sales and management strength of the organization. Major additions were made to the facility on West Water Street in 1977, 1983, 1986, and 1987. In 1981 a warehouse at 3115 North 21st Street was purchased

Nemschoff found that its entrance into this business was very timely. There was a definite need for a manufacturer that could produce good design and quality, along with the ability to modify the products to meet the needs of designers and architects—a flexibility not readily available from larger manufacturers.

New college building programs and refurbishing projects on many campuses also presented a great opportunity for Nemschoff Chairs. The building owners preferred to refurbish with new lines so that the buildings would look fresh. In developing this new product line, Nemschoff carefully introduced designs that could blend with a number of established lines so that the products could be used

Skilled workers assemble a variety of Nemschoff products that compete in the international marketplace.

and converted for the manufacture of cabinets, storage cases, and allied products. Major additions to this facility were made in 1982, 1984, and 1987.

With the addition of this product line to complement the established seating and table line, Nemschoff became a new force in the institutional furniture market. Today Nemschoff Chairs represents the broadest product line available for that market. Throughout the expansions careful attention was paid to ensure flexibility and responsiveness to the special needs of the varied institutions. In addition to the broad standard

product line, approximately 50 percent of production is devoted to specialized products or modifications of standard products.

To accomplish this versatility and maintain its reputation for service and quality, the company is involved in a constant program of updating technology. When these needs cannot be met by existing equipment or published information, Nemschoff finds solutions within its own group of highly skilled employees. The firm has made significant contributions to the development of problem-solving products, production equipment, and data-processing programs. The industry recognizes Nemschoff as an innovator in products and marketing. The company's QP program, a controlled system for the quick passage of orders from receipt to shipment, has enabled Nemschoff to sustain growth with reasonable inventories. It has also brought the firm's many good suppliers and service sources into a very close teamwork effort.

The key to Nemschoff Chairs' accomplishments lies with all 350 of its dedicated, loyal, and informed employees. They, along with the company, survived the long, uncertain period in the 1960s by coping with constant change, applying the very latest technologies, and producing products that compete in an international marketplace. The firm recognizes the need for continuing education and joins its employees in pursuit of that effort. It supports both the Upholsterers International and United Furniture Workers unions, which have maintained agreements with the company from the beginning. The personal partnership with management ensures the security of Nemschoff Chairs, Inc., and its employees.

THE TORKE COFFEE ROASTING COMPANY

The Torke Coffee Roasting Company is an outgrowth of the Sheboygan Coffee Company, a house-to-house concern. In 1941, the company was converted to a commercial coffee roasting firm.

Today the company is a leading regional roaster of select coffees and an assembler of fine teas. Presently, the firm is celebrating its 47th consecutive year of growth.

Distribution of Torke products is through a fleet of company trucks, dealers, and food purveyors.

With the benefit of planning and architectural assistance, strides were accomplished resulting in the location of the principal offices and plant to 3455 Paine Avenue, in the Sheboygan Industrial Park.

At this location a new modern high-speed coffee processing plant, employing the latest technology, was installed. The results are efficiency together with the coffee untouched by human hands from green, to roasted, ground, and packaged form. The plant is highly rated and has had visitors from throughout the United States and Canada.

A further development includes a market system with a satellite screen displaying constant action of the New York coffee, sugar, and cocoa exchange during trading sessions. Further support includes a constant printout of world events.

The acquisition and supply of green coffees includes shipments from North America, Central America, South America, Asia, Africa, and other coffee growing areas, with delivery through the ports of New Orleans and New York, and also via Laredo, Texas.

A new and enhanced computerized system and testing room permit greater selectivity in the production of fine aromatic coffee and exceptionally pleasant drinking teas.

Research and development continue to play a large part in the production of Torke coffee and Torke teas. Currently, plans are under way for further expansion

A new high-speed coffee processing plant and offices were established in the Sheboygan Industrial Park.

Forty-seven years of growth.

THE STUBENRAUCH ASSOCIATES, INC. ARCHITECTURE, ENGINEERING, PLANNING

Few architectural firms enjoy the privilege of celebrating 67 years of continuous service to their community and state as does The Stubenrauch Associates, Inc.

The founder of the firm, Edgar A. Stubenrauch, is a native of Sheboygan and a product of its public schools. Upon completion of his degree in architecture, Stubenrauch enlisted in the U.S. Army and served two years in France. Before leaving Europe he attended London University for six months. When he returned to the United States he was employed by the State Architect of Wisconsin for two years. Having completed his internship, he returned to Sheboygan and opened his own office in 1921.

His first office was on the second floor of the Pfister Jewelry Store, his first major project was The Sheboygan Clinic. The clinic building created a great deal of interest because it was the first reinforced concrete frame structure to be built in Sheboygan. Soon after that Stubenrauch designed the Rocky Knoll Sanitorium near Plymouth. In 1928 he supervised construction of the Bowler Building, and, upon its completion, he moved his office to the second floor.

With good management and aggressive efforts in business development, the firm managed to survive the Great Depression of the 1930s and the wartime setbacks to keep its doors open for service to the people and communities of Wisconsin. One of the major architectural plans produced at that time was a 250-unit housing project at the Manitowoc Submarine Base. Also during the 1940s Stubenrauch purchased a large residence at 712 Erie Avenue, and the

Great interest was generated as The Sheboygan Clinic went up in 1921. It was the first reinforced concrete frame structure in the city, and the first major project designed by Edgar A. Stubenrauch.

office was moved to this location.

Edgar A. Stubenrauch continues as director emeritus of The Stubenrauch Associates, Inc. Fred Steinhaus, also a director emeritus, joined the firm in 1927 and served until 1985. His leadership

role included secretary, president, and chairman of the board. He helped create and design many notable Sheboygan landmarks, such as the Citizens Bank of Sheboygan, Urban and Farnsworth junior high schools, the post office, the Sheboygan Retirement Home, and many others.

In 1972 the firm's office was moved to a new building on the corner of Erie Avenue and North Seventh Street. Eventually branch offices were established in Appleton, Rhinelander, and Hayward to better serve clients throughout the state.

Today the organization's management is supported by a professional staff that includes specialists in design, construction services, value engineering, long-range energy planning, interior design, color coordination, interior furnishing, cost estimation, and administrative services.

Stubenrauch Associates' current officers are Norbert C. Schaefer, chairman of the board; H. James Gabriel, president; LeRoy Tislau, secretary/treasurer; and Henry J. Miles and Paul F. Dinkins, vice-presidents.

In its 67 years of fruitful production, The Stubenrauch Associates, Inc., has designed 330 churches, 395 schools, 363 housing developments, 214 public buildings, 186 health facilities, 377 industrial buildings, 80 banks, and countless other architectural projects throughout the state.

The employees of The Stubenrauch Associates, Inc., pride themselves on adherence to the principles of service, competency, integrity, growth, creativity, and contemporary designs.

The Sheboygan Retirement Home—one of the many Stubenrauch Associates projects in the 1980s.

VERIFINE DAIRY PRODUCTS COMPANY

At the turn of the century home delivery of milk was done by horse-drawn wagons, and housewives, using their own pitchers, bought as much milk as was needed each day from those wagons. It was during those early years that the Sheboygan Dairy Products Company got its start.

It all began when an Illinois man, Maynard G. Douma, came to Sheboygan and interested two local businessmen/brothers, E.C. Peacock (who ran Sheboygan Cold Storage) and P.H. Peacock (a cheese broker) in starting a butter and ice cream business. Two years later the fledgling company added milk to its line and made a revolutionary change in the sales process by putting milk in glass bottles and pasteurizing it for health protection.

Growth of the Sheboygan Dairy Products Company was so rapid that by 1916 it had outgrown its original quarters at 1018-20 Water Street, and had built a new three-story plant down the block at 934 North Water. Four years later a cold storage building was purchased nearby, as well as other dairy acquisitions throughout the state.

By 1923 Douma had bought out the Peacock brothers' interest, further expanded the Sheboygan-based firm, and added outlets at Green Bay, Milwaukee, and Monroe. Over the next 12 years other products were added to the company's line, expansions were made to the plant, and a modern name, "Verifine," was chosen for the new operation in Green Bay.

A year after the death of Maynard G. Douma in 1935, the board of directors of the Sheboygan Dairy Products Company officially changed the corporate name to Verifine Dairy Products Company, and Walter Grasse, Douma's son-in-law, became president.

Throughout the course of the next 45 years Verifine acquired numerous other dairy companies and went through changes not only within its production lines (at this time paper cartons replaced glass bottles), but within its management and ownership as well. When Walter Grasse retired in 1968, his sons—Robert, Richard, and W. James—became instrumen-

Sheboygan Dairy Products Company, shown in the 1930s at its Water Street location.

tal in running the business. W. James Grasse acquired 100-percent interest in Verifine soon after and, as president of the company, saw his organization become a giant among small, independent dairies in the State of Wisconsin.

Under W. James Grasse's leadership, Verifine's new production system of manufacturing plastic milk jugs became the first of its kind in the state. A few years later Verifine took another giant step in the dairy business when it floated a $400,000 revenue bond to proceed with a new venture—the plastic half-gallon milk jug. That same year Verifine halted its home delivery service that had started more than 68 years ago.

Now, 77 years later, with Tom Grasse (son of W. James) as president, Verifine Dairy Products Company takes pride in the fact that the name "Verifine" has always been synonymous with quality.

VALLEY VIEW MEDICAL CENTER

In 1914 the Reverend Martin Schmidt of St. John's Lutheran Church of Plymouth, Wisconsin, and his friend William H. Streblow, a retired farmer, enlisted the support of a small group of people, including city dwellers, farmers, and area physicians, to pursue their dream of a community hospital.

A committee was formed, and soon the group was canvassing the city and farming areas for stock subscriptions and donations. The location, a former cow pasture, was selected at the south end of Selma Street.

On November 1, 1916, the cornerstone for the two-story building was laid, construction was completed in roughly a year, and the

grams were produced. Donations of food and the hospital vegetable garden were also helpful. A growing population necessitated a fund drive for a two-story addition at the south end of the facility in 1927. A further addition provided a new obstetrics department and nursery, an operating room, and a new front entrance, as well as new

The cornerstone was laid on November 1, 1916, for the Plymouth Hospital and Training Center, predecessor to the Valley View Medical Center.

Increased demands for medical service made a new hospital necessary, and the new facility was opened in 1970. The name was changed to Valley View Medical Center in 1985.

new hospital was ready for patients. The name given to the facility was Plymouth Hospital and Training School. In 1955 a change was made in order to make the hospital legally eligible to receive memorial gifts: It became Plymouth Hospital Incorporated, a Memorial Corporation.

Community participation and self-help got the institution through the early years. While struggling to pay off early debts, plays and other community pro-

office space, lobby, conference room, two-story boiler house, and a laundry.

As the years passed the increasing demand for medical services made the commitment to an all-new hospital necessary. The dedication and laying of the cornerstone was held February 22, 1970. The new hospital building was connected to the old facility by means of an underground passageway. The old structure was then converted to an extended care facility for the chronically ill or for patients requiring long-term care.

In 1980 plans were implemented to build a new 60-bed nursing home, administrative of-

fice area, laundry, chapel, a 32-apartment retirement complex, and an activity center for senior citizens to the south of the existing hospital. Two years later the new facility opened its doors to the public. The extended care building was then converted to a professional office building now called the Brickbauer Professional Office Building. In 1985 the name of the institution was changed to Valley View Medical Center to better reflect the scope of services now being provided.

Today more than 75 physicians and 200 employees staff the Valley View Medical Center. The institution is accredited by the Joint Commission on Accreditation of Hospitals and provides all the services associated with a full-service medical center.

Valley View Medical Center provides all levels of care, such as critical, acute, subacute, and long-term care. The institution's diagnostic treatment and rehabilitative services include nuclear medicine, CAT scanning, ultrasound, cardiac stress testing, respiratory therapy, physical therapy, occupational therapy, speech therapy, a full-service clinical laboratory, medical social workers, pharmacy, and an extensive surgical department.

TRINITY LUTHERAN CHURCH

The top photo depicts the 1853 storefront and first place of Lutheran worship in Sheboygan. Trinity's first church building (bottom), on Eighth Street between Wisconsin and New York avenues, was acquired in 1854. The center shows the church from 1869 to 1882 at its present location.

In the early 1850s the Reverend L. Dulitz, a Lutheran pastor from Milwaukee, preached to Sheboygan's newest German immigrants in a local public school building. This led to calling the first resident Lutheran pastor to Sheboygan.

Otto Eisfeldt, an 1853 graduate of Concordia Theological Seminary in St. Louis, was installed as pastor of three Sheboygan-area German Evangelical Lutheran congregations: the Town of Herman, Town of Wilson, and the City of Sheboygan, where he made his home. All three were later named Trinity. Pastor Eisfeldt and 16 lay members organized the Sheboygan congregation on May 26, 1853, and also established a Christian day school. Both have been in continuous existence since then.

The first place of worship was located on the east side of the 500 block of South Eighth Street. Pews consisted of rough planks laid on blocks of wood. The altar was a wooden box covered with a white cloth.

Acquired in 1854, a former Presbyterian church located at the present site of the Mead Library served the growing congregation until the structure was destroyed by fire on October 5, 1868. That same day congregation members resolved to relocate at the northeast corner of Ninth Street and Wisconsin Avenue. The cornerstone for the Cream City brick edifice with two classrooms on the lower level and sanctuary above was laid in 1869. A frame school building, erected east of the church in 1886, was replaced with a red brick structure in 1914, which was enlarged in 1927.

Overcrowded classrooms resulted in the establishing of branch schools on the west and north sides of the city in 1877 and 1889, respectively. The churches built at these sites were Immanuel and St. Paul. Another daughter congregation, south side Bethlehem, was established by Trinity in 1890. All are affiliated with the Lutheran Church-Missouri Synod.

Through the efforts of several members, Lutheran Cemetery, adjacent to the city-owned Wildwood, was acquired by Trinity in 1883.

Until 1922 divine services were conducted in German. Bilingual services continued until 1974, when the last German worship service was held.

In 1968, 99 years after the original church building was erected, a comprehensive renovation program was undertaken. Completed in 1976, it included a gym and a connecting lounge between the church and the school.

Since 1976 Trinity has ministered to refugees from Southeast Asia. Several of these Hmong families have become active in the life of the church.

Church records as of October 1987 revealed that 17 pastors served Trinity since its humble beginnings in 1853, officiating at 11,342 baptisms, 7,940 confirmations, 3,367 marriages, and 4,896 funerals. Thousands of elementary school children received Christian instruction from 120 teachers. Church membership at that time was 1,939.

Trinity Lutheran Church has evolved into this imposing structure on Wisconsin Avenue.

ALDAG SHEET METAL WORKS, INC.

Jerome M. Aldag, owner and president.

Aldag Sheet Metal Works, Inc., of 3509 South Business Drive in Sheboygan, has grown into a $6-million business, and is recognized as a leading Midwest firm in the pollution/emission-controls and heat-reclamation systems field.

Aldag can best be described as a diversified mechanical, engineering, and contracting firm that specializes in industrial ventilation and pollution controls, as well as the fabricating and installation of industrial and residential heating, ventilating, and air-conditioning systems. The success of the company is woven from the threads of its ancestry—namely Ludwig Aldag, who brought with him from Germany his sense of business acumen as a journeyman harness-maker.

When Ludwig and his wife died, their son, Ernst Aldag, upon reaching a suitable age, became an apprentice blacksmith. By 1869 Ernst was proprietor of his own blacksmith shop and grocery store. Twenty-two years later he sold the business to his son, Ernst Aldag, Jr. Ernst Aldag, Sr., then became a hardware, heating, and plumbing merchant in Sheboygan at 526 North 14th Street.

In 1929, when Marvin Aldag, son of Ernst Jr., lost his job as an apprentice sheet-metal worker during the Great Depression, he started his own heating and ventilating business out of his three-car garage. Due to the growth of the company, it was moved to a new building at 1629 Union Avenue.

By 1946 Marvin had again moved the firm to a newly built

brick plant at 2126 South 17th Street. When the business outgrew those facilities, and expansion was no longer possible, a 12.5-acre tract of land was purchased off Business Highway 141. The firm moved into its new quarters in December 1968. Jerome and Kenneth Aldag, sons of Marvin, purchased the business from their parents in 1975.

By 1979 Aldag Sheet Metal Works, Inc., had grown into a $3-million-per-year business, utilizing 42,000 square feet of space in two buildings, including approximately 24,000 square feet of manufacturing area. Its annual payroll of slightly more than $2 million supports 70 employees. The company continues to incorporate the conventional small business principles of customer satisfaction and service, combined with engineering expertise.

As to the future, plans are under way to build a high bay addition to join two buildings together—Aldag's present headquarters and a recently acquired structure on an adjoining 5.5 acres

of property purchased from Jerome's cousins.

Jerome Aldag is the major stockholder and current president, and with his sons, David and Timothy; his stepson, Christopher Hill; and his son-in-law, Allen Dvorak, working at Aldag Sheet Metal Works, Inc., five generations of Aldags will be perpetuating a family tradition of excellence.

Aldag Sheet Metal Works, Inc., a diversified mechanical, engineering, and contracting firm that specializes in industrial ventilation and pollution controls, is situated at 3509 South Business Drive.

R-WAY FURNITURE COMPANY

In many respects, Sheboygan has played a significant role in the history of American furniture these past 100 years. Time was, Sheboygan was known as a furniture center because of its many manufacturers. A lot of those companies are gone now. One that isn't—and one that remains as renowned today for quality as it was years ago—is R-Way of Sheboygan.

R-Way traces its beginnings to 1881, when it was founded as Mattoon Manufacturing Company and located in Sheboygan Falls. The firm's president was George B. Mattoon—a man who first learned the furniture industry as a laborer in his brother's chair factory.

Aggressive and energetic, Mattoon eventually purchased the company and—recognizing Sheboygan's easy access to water transportation, proximity to fine northern timberlands, and attractiveness to skilled woodworking labor—soon moved the entire manufacturing facility to Sheboygan. Growth quickly followed, and with it came Mattoon Manufacturing's first building, a three-story structure where 35 workers manufactured bedroom and dining room suites.

Six years later disaster struck when a fire destroyed much of the plant. But Mattoon Manufacturing persevered, with its workers clearing away the debris, all the while on company payroll.

The 1890s saw Mattoon Manufacturing continue to grow. A 200,000-square-foot facility was constructed, and employment swelled to more than 1,000.

When George Mattoon died in 1904, many mourned his loss, but a new and even more exciting chapter in the history of R-Way was about to be written.

The man responsible for it all was Jacob L. Reiss, Sheboygan industrialist and entrepreneur. Born in Sheboygan in 1873, Reiss was a gifted business leader. At only 23 years of age, Reiss established the International Tailoring Company. Two decades later it was the largest made-to-order clothing manufacturer in the world.

On George Mattoon's death in 1904, ownership of Mattoon Manufacturing was assigned to a Sheboygan bank, which wanted nothing to do with furniture and had plans to liquidate the company (and, in effect, eliminate 800 Sheboygan jobs). Concerned for the economic well-being of his hometown, Jacob Reiss then stepped in to purchase Mattoon Manufactur-

R-Way traces its beginnings to Mattoon Manufacturing Company, which was founded in 1881 in Sheboygan Falls.

ing, and rename it Northern Furniture Company.

Success soon followed. In just five short years Reiss took Northern Furniture sales to more than one million dollars annually.

One of the keys to Reiss' success was his insistence on quality—and not just for Northern Furniture products. His was also an attitude of quality toward the people he employed, a trait that would become almost legend among his workers and future generations of R-Way craftsmen.

Another factor in Northern Furniture's success was a new and innovative distribution system Reiss instituted. By eliminating sales to mail-order and premium houses, and having salesmen call on dealers, more than 6,000 new accounts were added by 1909.

By 1910 Northern Furniture Company was the largest manufacturer of its kind in the world, employing more personnel, requiring more space, covering more territory, and selling more furniture through salesmen than any firm anywhere.

that in order to make the best products, companies needed the best people, working under the best conditions. As such, he put his philosophy into action, tearing down old wooden structures and replacing them with modern ones, expanding his factory space to 450,000 square feet by the 1920s.

His eye for improvement also included products. Under Reiss, Northern Furniture introduced American tastes to Chippendale, Sheraton, Hepplewhite, and Duncan Phyfe, just as Federal, Elizabethan, Louis XVI, and Queen Anne styles were popularized. In addition, when Jacob Reiss saw the need for marketing improvements, he made them, and over time people could actually see and feel and buy Northern's quality furniture in 10 company-owned showrooms across America. Throughout this period every Northern Furniture product was "branded" —on the inside of an upper drawer, the underside of a chair—with a trademark: R-Way.

While opinions differ as to the meaning of R-Way—some say it referred to "Reiss," others that it represented the "Right Way" of making furniture—one thing was certain: People looked for and looked to the R-Way trademark as a symbol of unsurpassed quality. By 1949 the R-Way trademark was so popular that Northern Furniture officially changed its name to R-Way Furniture Company.

When Reiss died in 1955, his impact on Sheboygan went far beyond a thriving R-Way Furniture Company. Among his many other civic accomplishments, his charitable nature contributed to the building of St. Clement's Roman Catholic Church, the Anna M. Reiss Home for the Aged, and an addition to St. Nicholas Hospital.

Descendants of Jacob Reiss

The legendary Reiss family quality standards are still a commitment at R-Way.

continued to lead the firm until 1962, when Franklin Industries of New York purchased the company, and shifted manufacturing emphasis from residential to commercial furniture.

For 25 years R-Way marketed its products to the office, college dormitory, and hotel/motel markets. Then, in July 1987, an R-Way legend was reborn and another chapter begun—a dramatic, almost romantic continuation of the saga Jacob L. Reiss started.

On that day Thomas Reiss, Jr., great-grandson of Jacob Reiss, announced that ownership of R-Way had returned to the family that operated the company for almost 60 years. It was an announcement hailed by the workers of R-Way, the community of Sheboygan, and the state of Wisconsin. And what a coming together of like interests it will be.

Thomas Reiss is chief executive officer of Reiss Industries of Watertown, Wisconsin. Reiss Industries is the largest manufacturer of custom-molded, "cold-cure" urethane components for the furniture industry and also operates, as a division, Watertown Table Slide Company, America's first manufacturer of table slides (primarily used in dining room tables).

Already, the legendary Reiss family commitment to quality is being seen at R-Way. Improvements have been made in facilities. The latest design and manufacturing equipment has been installed. And products? Not only are traditional R-Way products attaining levels of quality better than ever, but new and exciting quality products are being planned, for both existing and new markets.

"There's a special feeling in coming back to R-Way," Thomas Reiss says. "As Sheboygan can tell you, the Reiss family has one commitment: to be the very best, and make the very best. We make that commitment—today, and always —to our customers, our employees, and our community of Sheboygan."

JACOBSON ROST ADVERTISING

From upper left clockwise : Frank C. Jacobson, founder; Elizabeth B. Jacobson, cofounder; Jon Rost, current president; and Tryg Jacobson, chairman/vice-president.

Jacobson Rost Advertising is a full-service marketing communications agency with 30 employees and offices in Sheboygan, Wisconsin, and Providence, Rhode Island. Jacobson Advertising was founded in 1956 by Frank Jacobson, who, at the age of 35, left an advertising position with the *Sheboygan Press* to go into business on his own. Jacobson moved the family picnic table and its benches into his two-car garage at 1229 North Fourth Street, and Jacobson Advertising was born. Jacobson's first two accounts were the Burger Boat Company of Two Rivers and WaterCare Corporation of Manitowoc.

With Frank as the artist/ salesman; his wife, Elizabeth, as the writer; and Ruth Reed as typist, the infant agency began to grow. A year later, with Jack Stieber joining as an artist and production manager and Edwin Soffa as an artist, Jacobson Advertising incorporated.

The agency eventually required larger quarters, and it moved into a new 30-by-60-foot brick building at 529 Ontario Avenue.

In the mid-1960s Jacobson obtained the Sanna Dairy account worth well over one million dollars.

Shortly thereafter Jacobson also became agency of record for Kohler Company's generator division.

In 1972 Jonathan L. Rost, a copywriter and account executive with Carman & Associates in Madison, made the decision to move to Sheboygan and join Jacobson Advertising as an account executive.

Frank Jacobson, chairman, appointed Rost president in 1981. Tryg C. Jacobson, Frank's son, joined the firm six months later as vice-president. During the next

four years Jacobson Advertising doubled in size and added 2,000 square feet to its 3,600-square-foot headquarters. Capitalized billings grew in excess of $5 million.

The turning point for this financial increase came when the firm added the TREK Bicycle Corporation to its account roster. TREK's growth led to the acquisition of three more TREK subsidiaries. TREK eventually became the cornerstone for a new Jacobson subsidiary called The Sports Marketing Group at Jacobson Advertising. The credibility of the group played a fundamental role in the attraction of sporting goods clients based in California, Tennessee, Michigan, and Rhode Island. Two years later Jacobson established the Providence, Rhode Island, office.

In 1982 Jacobson Advertising won an ADDY Award (the Oscar of advertising) at the New York Advertising Club's annual competition. A year later Jacobson Advertising was elected to the American Association of Advertising Agen-

cies (AAAA). In the 1985 American Advertising Federation's regional Addy Award competition, the company received 30 awards, including 11 first-place Gold awards—winning more than any other agency in the competition.

As a result of a highly visible packaged cheese introduction in 1986 for Masters Gallery/World Wide Sales, Inc., the agency formed a marketing alliance known as the Grocery Marketing Group. The group is a consortium of companies that specialize in marketing, packaging, advertising, merchandising, and promotion for food and packaged goods manufacturers. Jacobson Rost currently works with more than a dozen such manufacturers and retailers under the Grocery Marketing Group banner. Jacobson Rost enjoys a reputation as being among the finest agencies in the Midwest. While creativity awards reflect Jacobson Rost's dedication to design excellence, developing creative communications programs based upon solid marketing principles has been the key to winning new customers for its clients.

With Jonathan L. Rost as president; Tryg C. Jacobson, chairman; and Beverly J. Rempe and Marc Braunstein, vice-presidents, Jacobson Rost Advertising today has annual capitalized billings in excess of $10 million.

WILLOWGLEN ACADEMY

Willowglen Academy appropriately named for its serene, willowed setting in Plymouth, is a residential treatment and therapeutic living facility for emotionally disturbed children and adolescents.

Willowglen Academy is a residential treatment and therapeutic community living facility for autistic, psychotic, and emotionally disturbed children and adolescents. Its ultimate goal is to return the children home, if appropriate, to function according to their capacity as members of society once they've found the key to unlock the bonds of their world, and enter into ours.

Willowglen Academy originated in 1973, when Dr. James Balistrieri and his colleague Donald R. Fritz from Milwaukee, decided to open a treatment center where a child could have his or her needs met in terms of education and therapy, free from a hospital atmosphere, and then progress to a less restrictive environment—be it theirs, a foster home, or a group home.

The corporation set out to purchase a facility that was in a rural community with a quiet setting. A one-story building with four acres of land that became available in the City of Plymouth at 1111 Reed Street fit their needs. A month later the new 10,000-square-foot, 26-bed treatment center began receiving children from around the state.

Within two years an expansion necessitated the purchase of a Milwaukee facility at 3030 West Highland Boulevard to accommodate children coming from that area. When the Plymouth facility became filled to capacity, a group home was purchased in 1977 at 109 Fairview Drive.

Through Willowglen's association with the National Society For Autistic Children and speaking engagements at various conventions, the academy's services became nationally known. Children from surrounding states and as far away as New Jersey—upon referrals from psychiatrists, psychologists, and other mental health clinicians—began arriving for treatment at Willowglen Academy.

As the academy's reputation grew, other buildings were acquired—one on Milwaukee's east side and another group home next door to the first Plymouth facility. In 1987 Willowglen opened a treatment center in New Jersey, since many of its out-of-state youngsters were coming from that area.

Today, in the three Wisconsin Willowglen Academies, there is a total of 149 beds and a highly trained staff of 180 people. Structure, control, and program continuity are fostered, not by walls or locked doors, but by enhancing ego development, improving personal functioning, and encouraging a healthy interpersonal relationship, both with peers and with staff.

Because of Willowglen's success and basic sixfold program, consisting of academics, recreational and activity therapy, prevocational training, group living, and therapy components, 30 percent of its youngsters, within a year's time (1986-1987), returned home or were discharged into some type of independent living situation.

Willowglen Academy's plans are to continue providing high-quality service through treatment and rehabilitation so as to enable each individual to maximize his/her own abilities.

Willowglen's group home on Fairview Drive in Plymouth.

VAN DER VAART, INC.

Dating back 100 years, Van Der Vaart, Inc., of Sheboygan is the oldest business of its kind in the community. It got its start in 1888, when August Zimbal and his son, Oscar, founded the Oscar Zimbal Brick Company.

The organization's first brickyard was located at the west end of New Jersey Avenue on the south bend of the Sheboygan River. Later, when the Belt Line (railroad tracks around the city) was laid, the original site was sold to the Chicago and North Western Railway. Oscar Zimbal then purchased 33 acres in the vicinity of South 15th Street and Georgia Avenue and built a new plant.

Following the death of August Zimbal, the firm was operated by Oscar for another 25 years. In 1926 John Van Der Vaart bought the business from Oscar and changed its name to Van Der Vaart Brick Company. John's son, George, was then made secretary/treasurer and general manager.

Three years later George

Though the equipment models change through the years, Van Der Vaart trucks remain a familiar sight throughout Sheboygan County and its surrounding communities.

The brickyard, which was the forerunner of Van Der Vaart, Inc., was founded in 1888. Today the company's main office and plant is on South 15th Street, Sheboygan.

started building a pipe plant to produce concrete pipes for sewers and culverts. In 1931 the stockholders of the Van Der Vaart Brick and Building Supply Company met and formed the Wisconsin Concrete and Culvert Company.

Upon the death of George Van Der Vaart in 1932, Louis Gartman became vice-president. Four years later he was named president following the death of John Van Der Vaart.

As the business continued to expand, Van Der Vaart purchased the Wiegand Concrete Products Co. of Green Bay in 1944 and renamed it the Wisconsin Concrete Products Company. When Louis Gartman died a year later, Royal Fenn became manager of the organization and continued to serve in that capacity even after the firm was sold to the Paulys of Manitowoc in 1945.

Following World War II Van Der Vaart abandoned the brick-manufacturing business and tore down the kilns. In ensuing years a newer and larger plant was built at the South 15th Street location, and other acquisitions were made consisting of a central ready-mix yard at 2215 Calumet Drive, Vogel Brothers Excavating in New Holstein (now Tri-County Ready-Mix & Excavating), and the Sheboygan Brick Company.

In 1986, when Michael Harvey of Sheboygan Concrete in Sheboygan Falls acquired the Van Der Vaart Brick and Building Supply Company, he changed its name to Van Der Vaart, Inc. The Harveys have been in the ready-mix business for more than 50 years with plants in Manitowoc, Sturgeon Bay, Two Rivers, and Sheboygan Falls. The company was founded by Charles F. Harvey, who is still active at the Manitowoc plant. Charles' sons, Michael, Pat, and Reed, are all active in the business. Within a year a new office building was constructed at the South 15th Street plant. In addition to the main plant, Harvey has consolidated Sheboygan Concrete and the C. Harvey Company of Manitowoc under the Van Der Vaart umbrella.

A century ago the Van Der Vaart Brick Company was engaged in the manufacture of common brick. Today Van Der Vaart, Inc., not only employs 125 people and operates 25 ready-mix trucks, but also supplies a complete line of ready-mix and building supply materials to its customers throughout Sheboygan County and its surrounding communities.

PRIGGE'S DISCOVERY COACH LINES

John Prigge and his bride, the former Lucille Trossen, moved to Sheboygan from Centerville in 1925. John secured employment at the Blue Arrow Auto Laundry at 917 North Ninth Street. For 14 years John worked for Wensel Marsch, who owned the Auto Laundry and Marsch Bus Service. In 1939 he purchased the Auto Laundry, which he operated until 1960, for $200.

In 1948 John contracted with area funeral directors to manage their auto and hearse service. In 1949 John and his son Jerome purchased a new ambulance and established Prigge Ambulance Service. They also purchased Marsch Bus Service, which operated two motorcoaches and one school bus.

In 1950 they contracted with the Sheboygan School System to transport rural students to school. Today they continue to transport all the Sheboygan School District's rural and special education children.

In 1956 John's youngest son, James, took over his father's half of the business. Jerry and Jim as-

John Prigge, founder.

sumed responsibility for the school and charter bus operation. John operated the funeral service until he retired in 1962.

The company purchased the Diamond T Truck and Service Garage at 930 North Ninth Street in 1960 to use as its bus garage. In 1963 the firm purchased Glenn's Brake Service, located next door.

These facilities served as the company's office and repair garage until 1974, when it purchased a 2.5-acre parcel of land along South Commerce Street. In 1975 the firm acquired Clicquennoi Body Shop on the corner of Pennsylvania and Commerce. The building was converted to corporate offices, and a 10,000-square-foot service facility was constructed across the street.

Discovery World Travel was opened in January 1976 to coordinate the sales of motorcoach tours and provide airline, cruise, and railway packages to the public. Branch offices in Plymouth, Fond du Lac, and Port Washington were added in 1977, 1984, and 1985, respectively.

Riverside Truck and Auto Supply began operations in 1977, in a new structure built along the Sheboygan River. Riverside was established to provide automotive supplies for the firm and the general public. In 1985 and 1986 branch stores were opened to serve the north and south sides of Sheboygan.

In 1987 the corporation purchased the Chicago and Northwestern Railroad Depot on Depot Street. The building is being restored to its original beauty.

Also in 1987 construction was begun on a 42- by-115-foot building to house a new service center on Depot Street. This facility was named the Depot Car Care Center.

The multicorporation employs over 125 people and operates more than 90 vehicles at nine locations within a 40-mile radius of Sheboygan. Its years of dedication and commitment to its clients provide a firm foundation for many years of quality service.

Prigge's first Diamond T bus in 1940.

PATRONS

The following individuals, companies, and organizations have made a valuable commitment to the quality of this publication. Windsor Publications and the Sheboygan County Chamber of Commerce gratefully acknowledge their participation in *Sheboygan County: 150 Years of Progress.*

Aldag Sheet Metal Works, Inc.*
Alumaroll Specialty Company Inc.
American Orthodontics Corporation*
Ametek, Inc.
    Plymouth Products Division*
William A. Bahr, C.F.P.
Ballhorn Chapels, Inc.*
Bemis Manufacturing Company*
Burkart-Heisdorf Associates, Inc.
The H.C. Denison Company*
Eclipse Manufacturing Company*
First Interstate Corporation of Wisconsin*
First Wisconsin National Bank*
First Wisconsin South West Bank*
J.L. French Corporation*
Heritage Mutual Insurance Company*
HMF Inc.
Jacobson Rost Advertising*
Kieffer & Co., Inc.*
Kohler Co.*
Lake to Lake Dairy*
Marathon Integrated Data

Systems, Inc.
The Mayline Company*
K.W. Muth Company/Muth Wood-Stock Company/ American Wood-Stock Company*
Mr. & Mrs. David Arthur Neese
Nemschoff Chairs, Inc.*
Pemco Company*
Plastics Engineering Company*
The Polar Ware Company*
H.C. Prange Company*
Prigge's Discovery Coach Lines*
Richardson Industries, Inc.*
Rindt Enterprises*
R-Way Furniture Company*
St. Nicholas Hospital*
S&R Cheese Corporation*
Sargento Incorporated*
Jos. Schmitt & Sons Construction Company, Inc.*
Schreier Malting Company*
The Schwarz Fish Company*
Security Travel, Inc.
Sheboygan County Abstract Company
Sheboygan County Historical Society
Sheboygan Memorial Medical Center*
Sheboygan Paint Company*
The Sheboygan Press
The Stubenrauch Associates, Inc./ Architecture, Engineering, Planning*
Thomas Industries, Inc.*
The Torke Coffee Roasting Company*
Trinity Lutheran Church*
Valley View Medical Center*
Gerald R. Van De Kreeke, CPA

Van Der Vaart, Inc.*
Verifine Dairy Products Company*
Village Realty & Development
Vinyl Plastics, Inc.*
The Vollrath Company*
Watry Industries, Inc.*
Weaver's Inc.*
Wigwam Mills, Inc.*
Willowglen Academy*

*Partners in Progress of *Sheboygan County: 150 Years of Progress.* The histories of these companies and organizations appear in Chapter 8, beginning on page 137.

BIBLIOGRAPHY

Books

Arpke, Jerome C. *The Lippe-Detmolder Settlement in Wisconsin.* Milwaukee: Germania Publishing Company, 1895.

Buchen, Gustave W. *Historic Sheboygan County.* Reprinted and indexed, 1976. Sheboygan, 1944.

History of Northern Wisconsin. Chicago: Western Historical Company, 1881.

Jaberg, Eugene C. *A History of Mission House Lakeland.* Philadelphia: Christian Education Press, 1962.

Joerns Brothers. *Illustrated Historical Atlas of Sheboygan County.* Sheboygan: Joerns Brothers, 1902.

Reiss, Jacob. *Jacob L. Reiss: An Autobiography.* Private Printing, 1937.

Vollrath, Jacob. *Vollrath Family History.* Private Printing, 1980.

Newspapers

Evergreen City Times, Sheboygan
Intelligencer, Green Bay
Milwaukee Journal, Milwaukee
National Demokrat, Sheboygan
Plymouth Review, Plymouth
Sheboygan County News, Sheboygan Falls
Sheboygan Daily Journal, Sheboygan
Sheboygan Press, Sheboygan
Sheboygan Times, Sheboygan

Letters

Charles Cole
Mary Cole
Daniel Hyatt
Phillip Kasper
Dr. Elisha Knowles
Laura Chase Smith

This 1867 bird's-eye view of Sheboygan shows the city clustered around the harbor and river with many sailing vessels near the port. The point of land jutting into the lake in the upper right hand corner is "North Point" site of the lighthouse.

INDEX